Be The Chocolate Milk

Successful Selling For Homogenized Professionals

By Chris Whalen, CPA

Published by Christopher R. Whalen

Library of Congress Control Number: 2018911748

ISBN: 9780979352263

www.bethechocolatemilk.com

This book is dedicated to my many teachers and mentors. Some of the most important are listed below. From shared childhood bedrooms to the borough of Queens, from New York alleyways to the inside of classrooms, they educated me through the use of textbooks, biographies, newspapers, documentaries, annual reports, and face-to-face encounters in my personal and professional life. Without them, I would still only be a wee pint of regular milk in a dairy case, surrounded by a million identical bottles.

Mary Franklin

James Whalen

T.J. Brown

George Rademacher

Anthony Love, CPA (the real one)

Renee McSorley

Lee Merendino, CPA

Joseph Dwyer (JOED!)

Tyler Wands

Philip Dennis, CPA

Marcia Kalman

Also by Chris Whalen, CPA

Foxhole Father, The Field Guide for Fathers

Do you have examples of how you strive to "*Be The Chocolate Milk*" every day? I'd like to hear them!

Please write to me and tell your story at

info@bethechocolatemilk.com.

Thank you,

Chris Whalen, CPA

"WHATEVER YOU DO, DO IT WITH ALL YOUR MIGHT. Work at it, if necessary, early and late, in season and out of season, not leaving a stone unturned, and never deferring for a single hour that which can be done just as well now. The old proverb is full of truth and meaning, "Whatever is worth doing at all, is worth doing well." Many a man acquires a fortune by doing his business thoroughly, while his neighbor remains poor for life, because he only half does it. Ambition, energy, industry, perseverance, are indispensable requisites for success in business. Fortune always favors the brave, and never helps a man who does not help himself."

— P.T. Barnum

Foreword

I had the pleasure of meeting Chris Whalen, CPA when we were both working as junior accountants at a local mid-sized CPA firm. On that fateful day in 1990, Chris told me we would be friends forever. Apparently, he was right, as 28 years later that sentiment still holds true. Friendships like ours are few and far between, and even more scarce among business colleagues.

Having known Chris for so long, I had the opportunity to watch as he left the firm and started his own CPA practice, literally with a desk and a computer in his basement. Over the years I was able to observe him grow his business into a very successful one, literally from the bottom floor up. He wasn't handed his business; he never bought out anyone else's clients, nor did he take the partnership track. His business was built from scratch with his own hard work, one client at a time. Trust me, Chris is a hard worker. He not only provides tax and accounting services to his clients, he also does extensive blogging, podcasts, online interviews, seminars, and radio interviews. And on top of that he is the loving father of three beautiful children, and found the time to write another book, *Foxhole Father, The Field Guide For Fathers.*

However, hard work does not always translate into a successful business. Nor does working the longest hours, or being the smartest. Being able to rise above the competition takes a special set of tools at your disposal, especially when what you're selling is hard to differentiate from what the competition has. I was lucky that my friend shared his tips and procedures with me, and even gave me the blueprint to quit and start my own CPA business.

Over the years I have had the opportunity to work with my friend and have relied on his sage advice many times. We all know that getting customers, managing their expectations, and running a successful business is no easy task, and that's the whole purpose of this exciting new book. Within, he shares with all of us the elements that will help you rise above the competition and to be the best out there so that customers will want to work with you above anyone else.

In this book, you will learn that it is not just price that attracts customers. In fact, getting into price wars is counter-productive. By reading this book and following the author's advice, you will understand how to get clients, how to treat clients, how to bill clients, how to deal with them, and when to let them go. Letting clients go can be the most difficult part of any business, but it doesn't have to be. Chris will explain why you should be happy to see some clients go. But this book is so much more than just that. Chris shares with us his everyday tips for a smooth-running office, including simple policies that will keep your work flowing fast and bring in the profits. After all, isn't that why we are in business?

Chris also shares many of his technology and time saving tips. I'm sure everyone can benefit from the chapters that will teach you how to speed up the mundane tasks in your day. My personal favorite is the chapter on how to increase your typing speed. I wouldn't have believed it had I not tried it myself. The book is worth the price for that chapter alone, and the solution is so simple. That chapter is just one of many time savers included in this book.

Who hasn't heard the phrase, "Time is Money"? Well, that might be true, but time is so much more important than that. After all, time is all we have on this earth to give. Therefore any actions you can take to simplify or speed up a business process is a worthwhile investment. And this book is set up to save time itself. The chapters are set up as individual topics that can be easily referenced from the index. Read them all and then quickly refer back to them whenever you need a refresher. If all that isn't enough, there are also the chapters on quality-of-life issues. After all, working to be the best you can be in business is not all there is to life. You will want to enjoy the fruits of your labor with a peaceful mind. Learn how to identify toxic relationships, both business and personal, that merely serve to drag you down and keep you from playing your "A" game. This book covers it all from A to Z.

In conclusion, I highly recommend this book for anyone in business. It doesn't matter if you are selling apples on the corner or high-end machinery, everyone wants to be the best. Whether you are just starting out or are the CEO of a major corporation, this book will give you the tips and advice you need to be the top dog out there—to "*Be The Chocolate Milk*."

Anthony Love, CPA (The Real One)

Table of Contents

Marketing

Mindset/Philosophy/ Quality-of-Life Tools

Client Specific

Actions/Processes

Technology

Business Administration

prodserv(TM)

Prodserv? Is this a typo?

During my writing of *Be The Chocolate Milk*, I found many instances where I needed to say "product or service." It began to sound repetitive and wordy.

So I created a word, prodserv, as a substitute to simplify reading.

For example, instead of writing "People must have faith in you before they will have faith in your product or service," I wrote, "People must have faith in you before they will have faith in your prodserv."

What Is a Homogenized Professional?

A Homogenized Professional is anyone selling a non-unique (homogeneous) prodserv. It is that simple. I'm a great example of a Homogenized Professional.

I am a Certified Public Accountant who prepares taxes and specializes in business consulting. I am surrounded by countless other CPAs who provide similar services. Other examples of Homogenized Professionals are lawyers, doctors, office equipment salesmen, mortgage and insurance reps, custodial supply salespeople, and oil change franchisees.

Are you a Homogenized Professional? How do you know? Simple. Do many companies sell the same prodserv as you? At first glance, or even at second glance, is it extremely hard to differentiate between you and the competition? If so, you are a Homogenized Professional.

One of the best analogies to explain this concept is types of milk. Vitamin D whole milk is a homogeneous commodity. And that is how many of us feel about what we're selling. This book aims to change your perspective so you can change your clients' perspective and increase your sales.

Imagine a dairy case filled with several gallons of whole milk and one gallon of chocolate. Your eyes instantly go to the chocolate milk, your taste buds want the chocolate milk over the regular milk, and you're willing to pay more for the chocolate milk because of a real—not just perceived—value difference.

This value difference is what the Homogenized Professional needs to strive for with his or her homogenous prodserv.

Be The Chocolate Milk can help transform you from regular whole milk to chocolate milk.

Let's get started.

Marketing

1

The Emotional Intensity of Client Need

The sooner you address a client's concern, the more emotionally impactful your solution will be. Your goal should be to maximize this positive impact and capitalize on it. As each moment passes that you haven't provided a solution or even a response to a client's need, this positive emotional impact opportunity quickly dissipates. It is then replaced by feelings of disillusionment and abandonment, which will quickly intensify within your client.

The graph below attempts to visually demonstrate this.

The heart is at (0,10). It is the initial moment your client has a need. This is the moment you want to capitalize on. The client's emotions are the most elevated. You want to insert yourself as close to (0,10) as possible and let your client know you are on the job for them.

The Y Axis is Emotional Intensity from zero to ten.

The X Axis is Days Passing, one through ten.

The dotted line is Emotional Intensity of the client need over time. As time passes, this usually subsides.

The dashed line is Abandonment Intensity felt by the client over time. As time passes this increases. This line also represents the Probability of Client Loss.

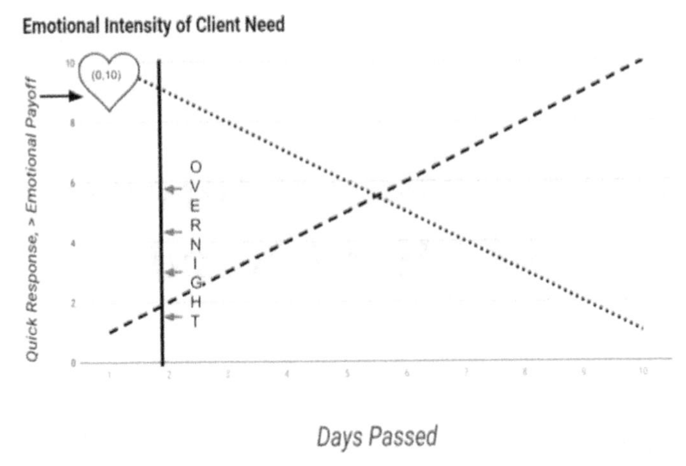

Please note the black vertical line just before day 2 is reached. This line is very important. Addressing a client's concerns prior to them having a full night's sleep is critical. After a full night's sleep most clients will have a more measured perspective on any unresolved issue, so the impact of our providing a solution is diminished.

I realize you may not be able to provide a full solution on such short notice, but contacting the client as soon as possible is still vital. Inserting your solution (prodserv) within this initial emotionally heightened client space will increase your client's allegiance to, and reliance on, you.

We have all heard the phrase "If you snooze, you lose." I always say, "The client kept, has not slept."

Incorporating this strategy into your daily business life can bring great rewards.

This is a great way to build customer allegiance and a deep emotional bond with a client that can span years of time. Also, a client is much more likely to refer you when you have impacted them emotionally and not just materially.

The sooner you provide solutions, the less likely your competition has the chance to move into your client's emotional and physical space.

The longer you wait to provide solutions, the more likely your competition is to provide an alternative.

But, if you take my advice, you will resolve the client's problem in the shortest possible time, and your competition will not have that chance.

2

Become an Extension of Your Client's Mind

BTCM (Be The Chocolate Milk) *Mindset/Philosophy/Quality-of-Life Tools* #27 flows into this point.

Strive to become an extension of your client's mind and heart, not just someone sitting across a desk from them.

It takes a lot more than doing your job right to accomplish this.

How do you get there?

1. Availability/Response time. The sooner your skill set is available to solve client problems, the more integrated you become into client thought processes. You want your clients to feel you are sitting next to them, always ready to help.
2. Learn about your clients' goals, attitudes, fears, hobbies, ethnicity, and relationships.
3. Study your clients' prodservs and suggest where your prodserv can be of value.

Aim to understand your clients' modus operandi and their emotional basis for their business actions. These are never exactly the same from client to client.

If you can truly understand your clients personally, as well as their prodserv needs, you have a good chance of becoming part of their emotional and psychological space.

Now, when a client has a need related to your prodservs, he or she can use your skillset as if it was their own—no barriers or distance.

Becoming an extension of your client's mind increases client retention as you are now more than a vendor providing prodservs.

When I get a new client, I ask them about their relationships with other professionals/vendors. Quite often they feel like a nuisance when they need to contact them.

This is very common today, and I'm not sure why. Maybe people's stress levels are too high, and their clients are the victims of it.

A client may fear he is being nickel-and-dimed with billing, or she may feel she is not well received when she reaches out or when her calls are not returned promptly.

Always be extremely welcoming and openly appreciative, even if a client is calling to complain. Foster a pacifying environment where clients feel taken care of and never judged.

Ask your clients how you make them feel. If you go to a potential client meeting and do not get the work, humbly reach out to that person or company for honest feedback.

3

Managing Client Expectations Is Your Main Job

Managing client expectations begins with a detailed and clear engagement letter or contract signed by the client. If you don't have one of these, you are at the mercy of the client's whim when it comes to getting paid. Without these, the client's recollection may be enforceable. Remember, you are the professional and have the greater responsibility and burden of proof when dealing with billing disputes with the public.

Make sure your attorney has reviewed these thoroughly, and be sure they include verbiage that clearly states that if you are forced to sue the client for payment in the future, the client will pay your related legal fees if you are successful. I do not have the authority to provide legal advice, so make sure you have an attorney tighten up or add this section of language to your engagement letters and contracts.

Present contracts for signature in person whenever possible.

Get a deposit! You have every right to protect your financial interest. I request a retainer/deposit on the work I will perform, especially with new clients. A larger contract usually means more out-of-pocket expenses for you. Be sure to request a large enough retainer/deposit to cover your initial costs.

Charge interest—finance charges—after thirty days when an invoice is not paid. I use 1½% per month, or 18% annually. This is clearly written on the bottom of every invoice that I create and also in all of my engagement letters and contracts.

Under promise; over deliver. Sometimes a client has a valid reason to be upset about something or to ask questions about the job you've performed. However, even when you've communicated everything clearly and fully delivered what you promised, some clients will still complain.

Those clients do not stay clients for long.

Just because a client complains does not mean he or she is justified. I never assume that a complaining client is correct, but I do try to pacify them just the same. Take each case separately, never get defensive, suggest solutions, and move on.

Client expectations are very nuanced and emotionally driven all the time. There's no real way to quantify exactly what each client's emotional expectations will be.

If you don't personally understand the client, you are operating at a terrible deficit.

We have to craft our message along with our prodserv to make sure we are maintaining our clients' emotional and psychological expectations along with their prodserv expectations.

It is helpful to eliminate the potential for clients to be surprised by anything. Quite often when a client complains, something out of the ordinary has happened—something different from what they were expecting. That causes performance anxiety for them, vicariously through some action related to you. If you don't anticipate these things correctly, you can lose a client forever.

Always promise only what you know you can achieve 100% of the time. Too many of us get overly enthusiastic, and we want to deliver as much as possible as soon as possible. But our exuberance and good intentions can lead to disaster by misleading clients and not meeting expectations.

The client issues described here can seem like problems on the surface but are really a blessing. They provide the opportunity to strengthen client loyalty and perfect your systems.

Remember, wake up every day expecting conflicts. Don't let conflicts become setbacks. Role play them in your head, and have conversations by yourself in the car or shower to address fictitious negative situations that may come your way. This practice will change you from a deer in the headlights unable to put two words together to a calm and smooth leader who always seems to know what to say every time.

All of my advice will give you greater control over the entire sales process from initial client contact to screaming client complaints.

You should always have a client-based answer and solution. Make this a daily conscious goal.

4

People Assume You Can Do What Your Profession Requires

Sometimes it is a mistake to oversell the specifics of what you offer.

If you claim to be something, people will believe you until they find a reason not to.

For example, I have a full-service CPA firm. People will make many assumptions about this. The main assumption is usually "Oh, okay, he does income taxes." But they will also assume I can perform any other work they may have heard a CPA provides. I don't need to get into too much detail about what I can offer until they have a specific question. Instead I immediately begin learning about their needs. If they aren't asking enough questions, I ask leading questions to germinate some within them.

Let's say you tell me you sell toner cartridges. Instantly I assume your cartridges will print clearly and print at least the standard number of pages that the competition's product does. You don't need to tell me anything else, unless there is something special and different that makes your cartridges the Chocolate Milk. That might be a 20% greater yield in pages printed, or a recycling program where you give the customer ten dollars for each cartridge returned.

If I were selling toner cartridges, I would interview the potential client to assess current needs, first by getting an inventory of the make and model of every printer and copier the client owns. So the selling comes from the client, as you will hear me say far too often in this book, and I want them talking much more than me.

I would strive to know my top ten competitors in great detail so that when I ask the question "Where are you getting toner cartridges from now?", I will be ready with all of the ways my prodserv is better.

I have researched all of my possible competitors this way. I have competition that spans from the local non-CPA tax preparer with a sign on the front door of his house to the national firms and chains.

Back to *your* competition. What do they offer, and more importantly, what don't they offer? And what can't they offer? What is their pricing scheme? Is it transparent? Is it based in reality? How high is their turnover? How are they viewed in the Business-to-Business and Business-to-Consumer spaces?

Is the competition's prodserv superior to yours? If so, my advice is to transform your offerings into the industry gold standard, or if that is not possible, go and work for the company that provides the gold standard.

Never knowingly sell substandard prodservs. It is unethical.

You need to know as much about your competition as possible so you can confidently sell against their offerings and close every time. This is something I do every day. It will allow you to use your competition against themselves during sales calls. At the same time, if you focus on understanding potential clients and what their motivations are, your closing rate should skyrocket.

5

Only Share Specific and Original Content When Email Marketing

Only share original content and NOT too often. Rarely—or never—share others' content.

People feel a lot of pressure to post on social media and blogs. This can lead to oversharing and sharing substandard posts.

Provide real information that potential clients and your existing base can use. Never be selling; be educating. Never put out a generic newsletter unless it leads with something specific. Very few people read generic newsletters as they don't receive value from them. They are also often too long, and the print is often far too small.

Posts should be specific to one topic, timely, short, and effective. Your readers should come away having learned the value you offer beyond your prodserv.

All posts should be put through this prism and eliminated or reworked if they fail any one of these rules.

Your posts should detail substantive and specific work you are doing and the added value you are bringing to your customers! I love posts like that and would read them all day. I would then know specific times to refer business to you, which is the reason for posting in the first place. Generic email marketing and blog posts do not have this effect on influencers or potential clients. Generic emails should never get to my inbox.

A common generic post is a list of services offered. However, you may include a list of services at the bottom of a blog post whose topic was specific, as detailed above.

People appreciate original and specific posts. The more original you are, the more people will think of you as an expert.

Remember it's not the frequency of your posts but the effectiveness and originality of them that will get you traction and get you noticed.

There are so-called social media marketing companies that promise to do your postings for you. Many of them simply look for articles and other posts that relate to your industry or profession and repost them for you.

Please avoid this.

What do I do? I take the work and research that I'm doing for paying clients and develop blog posts to showcase my expertise. This might mean posting only twice per month. Drawing blog post content from current and specific work is more impactful than posting generic information or something that someone else created.

Sharing others' content is quickly ignored and is a marketing plan for the lazy.

It screams, "Don't listen to me! Listen to this more intelligent and savvy person instead!"

Many times unoriginal or generic content is resented by the recipient as today our inboxes are a monster to deal with. It is simply one more email they need to click the delete button to get rid of.

I believe there should be a ban on sharing generic information and reposting others' content. If I can't get the world to agree to a full ban, I will accept limiting these posts to a one-hour window, once per week. Then during the other 167 hours of the week we would only see solution-specific emails in our inbox.

On a Monday morning, as I am a half hour into managing my inbox and I come across one of these generic or unoriginal shared posts, I think, "Did you really need to send me the top chocolate chip cookie recipes for the holidays? Or the top five habits of famous people? Or the lists of insurance products you offer? Or a news article you did not write that may or may not relate to my business needs? Or did you need to bother me on a holiday when I am trying to escape work?

The answers are all no. If your posts are not being shared and therefore not starting a conversation, then your posts are simply filling up innocent people's inboxes and wasting everyone's time. If you are doing this, consider testing my method over the next few months to see if it has a positive impact.

I would rather get a popup ad that is based on my browsing history as that is much more targeted to my needs than generic emails.

How do you know if your posts are read and appreciated? How often are they shared, retweeted, etc.? How often do people write back to you thanking you for what you shared?

How many new client meetings do you get after each post or email? Are your subscriber numbers increasing or decreasing?

People will share posts they feel will bring value to others. I ask fans of my blog to send out my blog subscription link to others when they share a post of mine.

One of the first ways you can respect recipients is by having a subject line that clearly states what your email is about. Bait and switch artists are quickly hated and blocked. So, if you have a generic blog post, with a generic subject, do not send it. People will read and respect real information that can help them and resent the generic ones.

Avoid email subjects such as:

- Monthly Newsletter
- My Brochure Attached
- Accounting/Legal/Window Washing/Update

You get the idea . . .

Here are a few of my email subjects:

- Memo – If You Will Not Have Full-Year Health Coverage in 2017, Read This Memo Now
- Memo – Top 10 Tax Facts if You Sell Your Home
- Memo – Puerto Rico Hurricane Victims Tax Relief

I realize that not all of my blog posts are of interest to everyone. So giving them a clear subject line allows recipients to decide whether to delete or read. That shows respect. The open rate of my email marketing efforts (MailChimp®, Constant Contact®) ranges between 10% and 90%, depending on the topic. Email marketing companies provide analytics on your posts' performance. Learn what tools are available to you. If you don't use them, your marketing work is not complete.

If your posts are not leading to meetings, you need to rethink your strategy scientifically. That means test, test, and retest, and get feedback on your marketing plans before any wide deployment.

I would rather you do two original posts each week detailing your success stories and repost those a few times than repost someone else's content a hundred times.

To restate, do not overshare.

Some of you have compliance departments that are extremely restrictive. Also, there are some professions, such as attorneys and CPAs, whose advertising and posts are restricted by law. This is one reason why people see them as homogenized. You need to attempt to get your personal content and message approved for dissemination as often as possible. If not, then you may simply become part of the global white-noise. And no one wants to hear white noise.

So many things that come out of compliance departments are watered down and should never be sent to anyone.

Remember, you should be constantly thinking of customization and personalization when it comes to communication with clients and influencers. Very often, less is more. I would much rather see a message in a larger-than-average font taking up a half page where someone is telling me a true success story they had with a solution they provided than a full list of services they provide in three columns with miniscule print.

That is an email I will read and share. Most importantly, that real story will then be emotionally embedded in my psyche. This will ensure that when that situation arises with one of my clients, I will know who to call to fix the problem.

Isn't that what we all want to happen from our marketing efforts, especially with influencers?

You want potential clients to know you for very specific solutions to very specific problems. Posting about your generic services and products over and over again is a true course to failure.

I tell everyone that I welcome as many emails as they can send me in which they are teaching me in a case-study format about solutions they offer. These emails educate me and will help me keep that person in mind when I come across a client in the same circumstance.

Many times I look to other professionals for content from their disciplines and about their prodservs. I then create a blog post that will educate my networks and contacts. But this never takes the form of a sales pitch, and the other professional is not mentioned. For example, I may do a blog post about title insurance or about a commercial real estate closing and the nuances of those. These are information-based posts with useful tips the reader can use just like posts that I make regarding my business. This can generate a lot of goodwill from other professionals and influencers. How? When you get a call related to these issues and services you don't provide, of course you're going to forward that call to the influencer who provided you with the post's content.

Like blog posts and newsletters, marketing materials should be as brief as possible and always contain original and detailed information about the solutions you provide. Tri-fold brochures are rarely impactful and effective. Make them one page and easy to read from a distance.

Many marketers forget that people are using their smartphones more than desktops today. Why is this important? Quite often people use their phones to read their email and to browse the web. Desktop computers with a large traditional monitor are being used less and less. I format all of my blogs for smartphone viewing first, and then work backwards.

My memos are usually based on projects we have recently performed or research we have recently undertaken. My memos educate people for free. They give actionable information. I don't have sales pitches within them.

On a daily basis I get many new subscribers to my blog, and I am often complimented on it. This is something you should strive for.

6

Taking Business Cards Is MORE IMPORTANT than Giving Them

People form an opinion about you within ten seconds of meeting you.

It is much more important to capture potential client and influencer information than to hand out your business cards.

Most people will never look at your business card a second time.

What is my process for managing business cards received? How do I use them to their fullest marketing extent?

1. When I initially take a card from someone, I record a voice note on my phone if I feel there's important information I need to remember. I can transcribe this later and add it to my contact notes for that person.
2. If they don't have a card, that voice recorder comes in very handy. I will hit the record button

and ask the person to verbally give me their contact information. I always get their information, whether or not they have a card. The voice recorder icon is on my phone's main screen so it is always ready to be used.

3. In either case, I ask permission to add the person to my blog distribution list.
4. After a marketing/networking event:
   a. I scan in all cards received using an app such as CamCard. These apps OCR (Optical Character Recognize) the information and put it in the correct contact fields. It simply needs to be checked for accuracy. Imagine how much time that can save over entering in each business card manually. A clerical person or college intern can be taught to do this. Remember my rule: Delegate the clerical. These scanning apps allow me to capture an entire stack of business cards in quick succession, called batch mode. Then I go back and edit each one.
   b. Once all the scanning and editing is done, all of these new contacts are uploaded into my contact database automatically. I then go online and find a picture of each person to add to the contact record. Having headshots of all of my contacts is a great help in the long run. I always try to do this step while the people's faces are fresh in my mind. LinkedIn, Facebook, and company websites are good sources for these pictures.

c. Next I add each new contact to my newsletter/blog distribution list.

d. I send an email to all new contacts stating it was great to meet them and that I know I can find ways to build business together or provide a prodserv they need at this time. People I have met but who don't need a specific follow-up message can be sent this group email. In that email I make myself the recipient, and the contacts are listed in the BCC (Blind Copy) line. When I use BCC this way, the recipients will only see my email and theirs, not the entire distribution list. (Please note: It is very important when you email groups of unrelated people that you use the functionality of the BCC line. It is a mistake to use the CC line in situations like this, as all the recipients will then see a long list of other unrelated email addresses. That is unnecessary and unprofessional looking.)

e. For those people who will have a specific follow-up message, I send a personal email one at a time. I simply segregate those cards after scanning from the larger group and do the individual emails after my group email is done.

f. Finally, I set up FU (Follow Up) calendar entries for all significant contacts, especially influencers. See BTCM *Technology* #76 for more information on this.

Now let's discuss your business cards. They should be used as mini-advertisements. People love a show. I learned that from one of my first heroes, P.T. Barnum.

Here are the front and back of my business card. Please note how clear, bright, and easy-to-read it is, even from a distance. If you can't hold your business card in your palm and clearly read all the information on it, please consider redesigning it. Use fonts that are smooth, with no jagged edges, serifs, or ornately curved lines and that are spaced apart. Some fonts leave very little space between letters. The smaller the type, as on a business card, the less legible those fonts become.

Avoid confusing backgrounds on your business card. Dark backgrounds are usually a mistake. Multicolored designs only decrease legibility.

You must assume that people do not have 20/20 vision. Someone should not need to use readers (magnifying glasses) in order to clearly read your business card. That should be your goal here.

Here is the front of my card. If this book was in color you would see that my name is a bright hunter green.

Here is the back of my card. Please consider using the back of your business card as additional advertising. So many people have a blank second side of a card when just for a few cents more you can use that space to your marketing benefit.

(732) 673-0510

Chris Whalen, CPA

79 Oak Hill Road
Red Bank, NJ 07701
chriswhalencpa@gmail.com

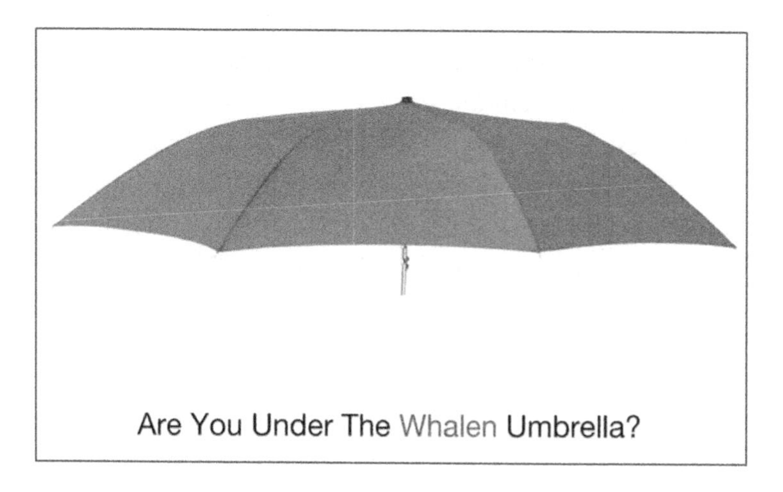

Here is how I sometimes use my business card to make a first impression. Again, the umbrella is a hunter green color.

When I give out my business card, I start to hand it to the person, but then I pull it back and lean in. This makes the other person lean in so we are suddenly in a more intimate environment. I will say, "From a tax and accounting perspective, I can tell that you are in a vicious storm. Do yourself a favor and make an appointment with me and get under the Whalen umbrella as soon as possible!"

And then I show them the back of my card, with the umbrella, at the very end of that little infomercial. This is all meant to make a greater impression than average and to become more memorable than others that person may have met during the networking function. I know this works, because people call me and tell me, "Chris, I need to be under the Whalen umbrella right away!"

It only takes about ten seconds.

Remember when first meeting prospects, this is your moment to make a great first and memorable impression. You sometimes only have a few seconds so try to devise a way to become memorable.

To restate the important takeaway of this chapter, it is more important to take business cards than to give them. If someone doesn't have a card, use a voice recording app to capture their information directly from them in real time.

7

If Your Superior Value and Service Are Not Obvious, You Are Trapped in Price Negotiations

When we first meet a potential client, many times we are perceived to be homogenized commodities like gallons of milk that should all cost the same. The client is not wrong, as their experience with your subpar competition has created this expectation. This leads to an almost immediate discussion and negotiation about your pricing.

But if you are selling your true value correctly, that should not last long, as they will soon realize you are The Chocolate Milk. Chocolate milk is seen as a unique and premium product. When you become The Chocolate Milk, you are no longer compared to your homogenous competitors.

When you become The Chocolate Milk, you are now a premium item. Think of prodservs you buy exclusively, regardless of price. You can achieve that status.

Your ability to impart your unique value coupled with unparalleled prodservs will minimize price negotiations. You must learn to not just do this, but to live this.

If you cannot do this, you will be trapped in price negotiations. Your profits will suffer, as you will have to charge the day's current "spot" price for your prodserv, the same way bushels of wheat are sold on a grain exchange.

This is a disaster. Don't let the market dictate your prices.

My definition of spot price:

> *"A spot price is the current price in the marketplace at which a given asset such as a security, commodity, or currency can be bought or sold for immediate delivery."*

Notice that definition does not mention value or superior service, as spot prices are not influenced by them.

If your prices are higher, and you have confidence that they should be, happily discuss this when the topic comes up and be prepared to answer why.

When I discuss my rates, people sometimes comment that they are higher than industry averages. I answer, "My value goes well beyond the services you are buying. Prior to our meeting you believed that my prodservs were homogenous commodities. I hope you will come to realize that with my firm, that is far from the truth. I believe I am the only one in my industry who offers what I do."

If you cannot get beyond price negotiations, then you may as well allow the client to tell you what they will pay you. This basically leads to you asking them, "What do you think my prodserv is worth?" You then have lost all control.

8

Sell (Care) FROM the Client: The Imperato Doctrine

My maternal grandfather had a fruit and vegetable business. He was my first business mentor and ran his business by three simple rules, which are the cornerstones of my business philosophy.

My grandfather's three steps to business success:

1. Sell the best prodservs.
2. Genuinely care about your clients' needs and best interest above all else.
3. Answer the phone.

These three steps are the core of my business model. I cannot stress enough the importance of these rules. Do you focus on these three things every day?

1. Sell the best prodservs.
    - You owe your clients technical excellence and product quality. Are you the most educated

in your field? Do you keep up to date with continuing education and become an expert in every new product you offer? Are you selling the highest quality products? Do you actually know if you are? If you are currently selling second-rate prodservs, suggest (strongly) to those in charge that they immediately improve quality to become the industry gold standard. If they refuse, go and work for the #1 firm. If you cannot honestly say you are selling the best prodservs, then you start out in a terrible deficit even before the sales call. This make you rely on deception-based selling.

2. Genuinely care about your clients' needs and best interest above all else.
   - This is self-explanatory. If you cannot sincerely do this, then finding true success may be impossible. Consider finding a career where you can feel this way with each client or customer.

3. Answer the phone.
   - I don't have a landline in my office. I want to reduce the distance between me and the client as much as possible. If I am in a meeting and I see a call coming in from another client, I will take it. Now, I will only stay on the phone long enough to give quick advice that helps them continue working. If

a client calls me, that usually means they are at a standstill and need my help getting back to work. At first, some clients get annoyed and feel disrespected when this happens, but they quickly learn that when I have answered the phone for them so often, I was usually also with a client. I want my clients to feel I am working for them alone. They quickly see the professional community I have created where I am a hub. They then will tell me to answer the phone when it rings during meetings with them as they begin to see the benefits for all of my clients. Less voicemails, quicker response, and keeping clients productive at all times are all components of keeping my clients' satisfaction levels extremely high. Answering the phone during meetings is a hard habit to start, as not taking phone calls during meetings or presentations is the norm. But to Be The Chocolate Milk, you need to be different in ways that buck the trends and provide greater value. This is one way I do that.

I urge you to get back to basics and make sure you are perfecting and living the three steps above.

Additional Steps Of Note:

1. Market and sell from the customer.
    a. Learn about your clients' families, hobbies, education, and long-term personal and profe-ssional goals.
    b. Emotions Drive All Buying Decisions

   i. What are your customers' true motivations? You cannot effectively sell them unless you understand them emotionally. You are selling the relief of an emotional burden, not just a prodserv.
   ii. No matter what you're selling—tax services, legal services, toner cartridges, ping pong balls, or plumbing supplies—your customers' motivations will vary in extreme ways.

c. Your greatest idea is only as good as the marketplace's opinions of it.
   i. Product and service development is too often started from the wrong direction. It should never start from you. The best new products and services grow organically by a combination of studying your client base and the market. Do both and you increase your success rate. Try to see all potential prodservs offerings through your customers' eyes, needs and wants, and never through your own vision. This takes practice. No matter how successful you are, the customer always knows best, and they must guide all new product and service development.

   ii. Urge your staff to make recommendations for new offerings and upgrades to existing ones.

2. Test, test, and retest.
   a. Don't offer any new prodserv without doing "limited exposure" testing. Limited exposure testing does not mean a minimum of testing. It relates to who the test subjects will be. We want that exposure to be limited, as negative reactions must be contained, managed, and learned from. Too much exposure during the testing phase could bring the same negative impacts in the marketplace as if you had done a full launch.
   b. I know this costs money and will delay the launch of prodservs, but there is nothing worse than testing your prodserv out in the wild of the free market.
   c. Do not let your desperation to get a prodserv to market cause you to make the mistake of beta testing something out in the free market.
   d. There is an exponential possibility of poor visibility and negative market exposure if you don't take the time to properly test everything.
   e. Many entrepreneurs and salespeople are high-strung and high-energy, and are seeking positive affirmation as quickly as they can get it. They may be slightly immature when it comes to this topic. I know I am! Take the time to pause and be deliberate.

3. Contain your exuberance and question your certainty.
    a. All too often prodservs are rushed to market out of a combination of emotional excitement, blind certainty, and over-confidence. You can almost guarantee success if you take a measured testing approach, and the opposite if you rush to market prematurely. Emotions can blind us and have us rush into things, the same way they do with regard to romance. So make sure you have a wise and stern chaperone at the table when you are "dating" your new prodservs. Over time you can become your own sober chaperone. Until then, hire one. This a great time to lean on a mentor. I elaborate on this in BTCM *Actions/Processes* #72.

4. Most clients want to be led. Show them you can solve their problems, and they will follow you.

9

No One Is Waiting For Me

You should be waiting on your clients as often as possible, not vice versa.

Of course in any business, clients are waiting quite often. But I want to make sure, especially during an information-gathering phase, that I am giving immediate attention to the account and alerting them to information I still need. If a week goes by and I suddenly realize there is information missing to do my work, I consider that an egregious failure.

Strive to manage clients' expectations to the point where their feeling of waiting for you is minimized. Of course we have deadlines and timelines and projected delivery dates. Try to do your best to manage those expectations, so even when a client is waiting they never have the feeling that you're late delivering. I cannot stress this enough.

When scheduling a call with someone always make sure to ask THEM to call YOU at a specific time. That way you can never be late to get on the call because you didn't have to make one. Again, you are waiting for your client.

Managing client expectations is one of the most important jobs you have. Make sure you understand the scope of your deliverables and be honest about delivery dates most of all.

Simply put, minimize late delivering and late responding.

With practice and forethought, you can achieve both of these.

This will elevate your client's satisfaction and retention.

10

Cultivate Your Client Base

Too often I see clients who ignore their client/ customer base as a source for referrals. Such a mistake! I urge everyone to analyze them to cultivate new business.

How do you do this?

Sort all of your clients in order from:

A+: I could not have invented a better client.

down to

F: If they left I would not be broken-hearted.

It is that simple. Look at your top 20% best clients. Then grade them using my scale.

Remember, birds of a feather flock together.

Who is consistently ordering from you? Who is paying their bills on time or ahead of time? Who seems to truly appreciate the value you're bringing? Which clients do you wish you could clone?

Develop a referral strategy and market to the top tier directly. It is worth your effort to spend this time. These clients have friends and colleagues just like them who are also in need of The Chocolate Milk.

Getting this type of hot lead is more beneficial than getting a thousand cold leads.

Getting existing clients to refer you is very nuanced and needs to be practiced and tested. Many clients for whom I am a consultant in marketing and branding services complain that their existing customers are not referring them enough. They make the mistake of believing that this is supposed to happen automatically.

Some clients and customers do not know how or when to refer a contact. It is wrong to assume they do. So instead of assuming you're being neglected, devise ways to broach the subject of getting referred, and make it positive for everyone.

You should not have to give extra incentives or discounts to your existing base for referring you. I also would not specifically ask for "five names of your friends and colleagues who I can contact." People are very protective of their relationships, and they will want to consult with their contemporaries before you make contact.

However, a satisfied customer should be happy to refer you to a colleague to do THEM a favor.

I simply say to an existing client: "I couldn't ask for a better client than you and would love a hundred more just like you! Would you do me a small favor? When you talk with someone who may need my services, would you ask them if they are happy with their current CPA?"

This gives them a very soft sell on your behalf. If the answer they get is "no," then the introduction is usually welcomed. My information is passed along and my phone rings shortly afterward.

Learn who your best clients are interacting with. Are they going to networking functions? Can you go as a guest? (I do this often). It is fantastic to be the only CPA at a gathering of a certain business segment. For me, getting many attorneys in one room is a great opportunity. Other great referral sources for me are contractors, real estate agents and brokers, etc. Who are yours? Take the time to develop a list and then a strategy to capitalize on them.

Who are your best clients' top vendors? Subcontractors?

Have you met the other trusted professionals your clients are using? I try to have a one-on-one with them as soon as I get a new client. They probably have many more clients who are in dire need of The Chocolate Milk.

Have you met and ingratiated yourself with you client's top staff? Key managers and employees are often an excellent source of referrals. Sometimes they spend more time in the field than the owner who hired you. Many times I interact with them more than the actual client.

11

I Hope People Are Questioning Your Pricing

If people never question your pricing, then you may not be charging enough.

This chapter may not apply to everyone. But if you're in a service industry where you bill by the hour or sell products you know are worth more than the competition, this applies to you.

All of our work comes down to getting a new client to sign on the dotted line. If you are at the stage where you are discussing pricing, you are 99% there.

At some point during initial conversations, ask for the client's budget and tolerance for cost.

When someone asks for your rates, answer quickly, clearly, and without hesitation. If you seem sheepish, much of the client's confidence may be deflated. If you don't act 100% confident in your rates, this will show.

It is very easy to get offended and defensive when people question your pricing, and this is a mistake. Avoid becoming combative. It is imperative to use the "Power of Pausing." Don't immediately react. Compose yourself, and filter your reactions "from the client" and not from you. Put yourself in their position.

The client has every right to validate the fees you are proposing they pay. It is your job to make sure they are pacified and believe they will get true value for every dollar they pay you. Their dollars don't have to wind up in your pocket. Never lose sight of this. Before you become The Chocolate Milk, you may still be a regular gallon of milk in their eyes.

Role play these types of conversations hundreds of times with infinite variations. Remember those early morning moments where I suggested you anticipate setbacks and negatives?

Most times it will be new clients who question your billing practices. Let's think about that, from the new client perspective. What information do they have? What has been their past experience with paying for services similar to yours?

They just met you, and their experience is with OTHER professionals or vendors in your industry. Remember, everyday people are buying things, and the pricing is consistent with relatively small variations. Think gasoline, milk, coffee, etc.

In my world, sometimes people have had a CPA for a very long time with only that billing experience to compare mine to. So most potential clients are coming in blind, and we all know that can breed anxiety and sometimes paranoia.

So, let's assume a new client who has no history with you has questioned your billing practices. Your initial reaction can be inordinate and over the top. But the reality is the client has asked a very simple question. Answer it politely and with true appreciation for the opportunity he or she is giving you.

On the opposite side of the coin, don't get caught arguing that your services are worth your fees. Certain people like to complain no matter what, and you can get stuck in a circular argument with no end. There are hagglers who shop price and already have a maximum price they will pay. The believe they are doing you a favor. Politely show them the door.

Price shoppers always wind up buying a generic gallon of milk for the lowest price and never The Chocolate Milk. We all know this is to their detriment, but we can't save everyone.

12

Influencers: The Most Underutilized and Uncultivated Sales Source

Influencers who have integrity will refer you, if you teach them when they should. Influencers can become rainmakers for you.

Integrity means that when you realize your client needs a function performed and you cannot do it, you recommend someone else to do it.

What is an influencer?

An influencer is someone who has the potential to "influence" others to hire you. Influencers have access to the same people and companies you want as clients. Influencers are a direct line to the clients you want.

A referral from an influencer is one of the hottest leads you can get. This potential client is usually the least concerned about your rates and will hire you based on your reputation and that strong recommendation. This allows you to charge what you are truly worth without haggling.

Most influencers you'll talk to do not have an immediate need for your service. Remember, once that initial conversation is over, you are out of sight and out of mind.

What is my goal with influencers? It is two-fold.

I want to be at the top of an influencer's mind in two specific situations:

1) When they are working for their clients and they need my input to continue.
2) When they need someone to recommend who can fulfill their clients' needs.

It is not enough to tell influencers what you do or what you sell.

Who are your influencers? Are you sure you know all of them? As an exercise, I urge my clients to prepare a list of every possible influencer they can think of. This is done as homework, and over the course of a few days or weeks. I then review that list and augment it the best I can. This gives us the initial demographic information to create influencer-specific marketing plans.

Remember, the lesson here is that it is not enough to give someone a menu or laundry list of the services you provide. Too many people take a generic approach to marketing their services to influencers. It is not enough for me, as a CPA, to let an attorney, who is a great influencer for me, know that I prepare income taxes.

Research your influencers and teach them how and when to recommend you. This is a very neglected part of influencer-based marketing plans. Internal influencers (your customers' employees with whom you interface) are as important as external ones.

If you want an influencer to recommend you, you must research and study the work influencers do. Explain in detail to your influencers where your prodserv should be inserted within their processes and work streams and those of their clients.

I'll give you a quick example. Let's say you are a commercial attorney and you have ten steps to completing a transaction for the buyer. Now, if you do those ten steps you are fulfilling your due diligence and professional responsibilities. But what if I know from my tax and accounting perspective that there is a step 5.5 that needs to be addressed with my skill set before you as the attorney can go on to step number 6?

See my point here? Once the client has been taught the significance of step 5.5 and knows that he does not have the skill set to properly address it, if he has integrity, he will have to call me so I can provide the answer. Then the process for him can continue on to Step 6.

Good tip: When you are doing work for an influencer or an influencer's referral, such as supporting a commercial closing I mentioned above, prepare an email to similar influencers in those areas and professions, detailing, in brief, exactly what you've done.

I constantly send emails and call influencers to let them know my firm is working within their sphere and professional areas in a supporting role.

I know this does not apply to everyone reading this, but take some time and try to see how your prodserv can be positioned within the workflow and work structure of other professionals or influencers you'd like to pursue as clients.

Many influencers do not realize where your prodservs are necessary and the value they bring to their clients.

Learn as much as possible about your influencers' profit centers, systems, production, and services. Learn the steps involved in as many of them as possible. Find out the key staff involved. Remember, key staff make recommendations to hire outside vendors all the time.

Look up the organization chart of companies. Put the key players in your contact database and make sure you target them as influencers as well. You will realize you have much more than one contact at an influencer.

As I have stated, lawyers are a fantastic influencer for me. Once I have sold the managing partner, I then get introduced to the other partners, then staff attorneys, office managers, and clerical people.

A 100-employee law firm has 100 potential influencers to send clients my way.

To learn about influencers for your industry, talk to them! Ask them when and how they use your prodservs for themselves and their clients. Talk to your mentors. I want you to trust me that this research and homework will be time well spent that can reap benefits for decades to come.

I would say that over 50% of my new business comes from influencers. I believe that is because I spend the time to do the research I have suggested you do.

My firm performs a lot of supporting functions for lawyers of all types. Remember there are many types of law: collaborative law, criminal law, commercial law, real estate law, family law, etc. I make sure every one of those attorneys knows what my firm can do to bring value and support to as many of their transactions as possible.

Prepare an influencer list as I mentioned above. Include not only the main contacts but also support staff. Then develop a strategy for each. Then test, test, and retest.

When perfected, deploy!

Clients' Office Managers and Support Staff

It is sometimes as important, or more important, to impress clients' office managers and other personnel than the owners, especially after you are hired.

As a CPA, getting a physician or doctors' group as a client is a great moment. But I have found that supporting and impressing their office managers is just as important as impressing the doctor/client. You'll find this with many clients. I sometimes interact with staff more often than I do with the clients during the year.

Consider marketing to those people directly, as I do. Office managers, controllers, CFOs, COOs, CIOs, physical plant managers, and bookkeepers are influencers within businesses, so I'm always looking for ways to promote my services to them.

Of course the thrust of my marketing stays the same. I will make their job easier, enhance their work and help them stand out, and provide a level of support they have never seen.

I find business owners don't market enough to influencers, and they especially don't market to internal influencers within their potential clients.

Are there any other people within the organizations that you want to work for or get as a client that you should talk to besides the owner?

Remember, entrepreneurs hire people to make decisions for them. So you may have an entrepreneur who never makes a decision about office products, or insurance, or accounting or marketing, etc.

13

Minimize Personal Comments and Questions In Your Professional Interactions

It is very easy to be seen as a sexual harasser, even for innocent and natural actions. Be constantly self-aware around people of the opposite sex during work time. That means all work-related time, not just in the office. This includes networking events, office outings, etc.

Today, asking a personal question can be seen as harassment. It is extremely easy to be accused of flirting and treating someone like a sex object for conversation that was considered normal banter just a few years ago.

A life can be ruined when a sexual harassment accusation is made, even one from decades ago. It doesn't matter if the accusation has merit or if there is any proof. The accused can lose his or her current job and never work in that industry again.

In a business setting, especially an office, keep interactions business-based and gender blind. Personal comments should be kept to a minimum and rarely go beyond common pleasantries.

"Good morning, Joan" is enough. "Good morning, Joan, how was your weekend?" is too much. This is especially true if the person is of the opposite gender. It is none of my business how Joan's weekend was. Today that simple question could be seen as harassment.

I used to advise clients to never say something to a person of the opposite gender that you wouldn't say to a person of your gender.

For example, I used to advise men to never mention how a woman looks, what she is wearing, how good her hairstyle looks, how great her perfume smells, or how much weight she has lost, because I would never say those things to a man. I would also say that I would never greet a man with a hug and/or a kiss, so I never greet women that way, either.

But now, with the litigious nature of the work environment, all non-business comments should be eliminated regardless of who you are talking to.

In a business setting, the only physical touching I employ are handshakes upon greeting and separating. I never initiate a hug, but I do accept them if offered to be polite. This should be the extent of your physical interactions in a professional setting. With coworkers handshakes are not customary on a daily basis.

There is never any reason to touch a coworker.

In today's day and age, even with great advances in gender equality, women are still the target of personal comments and touching in the workplace more than men are. But it is happening to men more and more. Eliminate these from your professional discourse. Any personal comment is now seen as potential harassment, even those that seem innocuous.

Most times these things are innocent, but now they are inappropriate, unnecessary, and dangerous during work time. These are things you may not be conscious of, so it is important to self-observe and exercise self-control when in the presence of the opposite gender. Be vigilant and make sure you are not misspeaking or touching someone. When around people of the opposite gender there is a natural, biological, and evolutionary tendency to become flirtatious. But we are not cavemen and cavewomen. That flirtation is regressive and destructive in the 21st-century business environment. Learn to control it.

To restate my easy rules:

1. Eliminate personal comments and discussions at work.
    a. Comments on someone's looks, scent, or clothing are never appropriate.
    b. Personal questions are unnecessary and potentially career-ending.
2. At client meetings or networking events, handshakes are the only acceptable and expected form of touching. If a hug is offered, accept only if you are comfortable.
3. With coworkers, no touching is appropriate, ever.

These rules may seem harsh, but today's business environment is treacherous and filled with hidden landmines. These rules greatly eliminate the possibility of being accused of harassment. Today, finding a way to be a victim makes people popular and gives them a feeling of self-importance.

All sexual harassers should be brought to justice. By following my rules, it is less likely that you will ever be accused of sexual harassment.

One caveat here relates to your interacting with clients. Depending on your profession, client relationships need to have a personal component. In my work as a CPA, understanding the clients' emotional and psychological makeup is very important as well as learning their life goals and personal and business struggles. Personal questions must be asked in that setting and are appropriate, if they stay focused on the work at hand.

14

A Simple, Consistent Message Is Easier to Remember

My message: "If we aren't working for you, you aren't working at your best."

Maintain consistent messages within your organization and in your marketing.

You want to become known for your message. So when you craft one make sure it's something your clients will be able to share with others as the basis of their relationship with you.

Look again at my message. "If we aren't working for you, you aren't working at your best." That is exactly what I want my clients to believe. I want them to believe they are 99% successful on their own, but unless they hire me, they cannot achieve 100% success and efficiency.

Sometimes companies make their marketing materials and websites too busy. There are too many messages, words, and images.

Today there are websites with sliding panels that go in every different direction. I find that this is a distraction, especially on the smaller screens of tablets or phones.

Make your website and marketing materials uncluttered and very clear. Do not be afraid of having empty space in marketing materials. That's exactly what I did with my business card. I hope you find it bold, welcoming, and uncluttered.

Visit this link to check it out:

Fronthttp://bit.ly/2z8zNdD

Backhttp://bit.ly/2z9chNx

Remember people have very short attention spans, and if they see something that's too cluttered or they hear a message that's too long and complicated, they will tend to ignore it or view it as chaotic.

I wanted to share a trick or methodology I use when I do professional reports. I also apply this to my marketing efforts.

When I'm doing a report that may go in front of a jury or arbitrator, I make sure to write it in a way that a disinterested third party, for whom English is not the first language, will agree with me and understand it when I'm done.

Take a few moments to think about that. Sometimes we are trying to overly impress with verbiage and flashy images when we really need to be simplifying our message to convey it clearly to a mass audience.

I apply this method always, even when presenting to boards of directors. Never assume that someone is sophisticated just because they have a certain title or position.

15

Answer Your Own Phone (Whenever Possible)

Remove obstructions in reaching you directly, and communicate in whatever way the client prefers. Today there are many ways that a client may want to contact you. I have clients who prefer to message on Skype or WhatsApp and never use texting or Facebook messaging or email.

Be sure to provide them access to you in whatever way they are most comfortable. Be sure to have those apps active on your phone and desktop at all times.

You will rarely hear these words: "Hold on for Chris Whalen, CPA" because I answer my own phone 99% of the time. When clients are in need, you want them to hear your voice as soon as possible. Eliminate all barriers between you and your clients. For example, I do a lot of work for law firms, and they still are under a communication paradigm from fifty years ago. It sometimes takes me three transfers to get to the person I'm trying to reach, and then sometimes I get the voicemail. This can waste up to two minutes of my time. That means if I refer my client to that attorney, they will experience the same issue, so I may hesitate to make that referral in the first place.

If another professional will not give me their cell number to call them, then I will not use them.

In your world, make sure that people can reach you as quickly as possible, especially when they are in need. You will hear me mention that time and time again. When someone is in need, even if it's a complaint, that is the moment where you build true client allegiance and retention.

I do not have a landline in my office.

My staff also answers their own calls directly. They use their cell phones. We can all choose to take a call or let it go to voicemail.

To those who disagree with me, I will explain the benefits. If you force callers to go through multiple layers (main switchboard, then an assistant or secretary), and if you are not available, the caller will go to voicemail anyway—or even worse, leave a physical message to be seen by you at some later time.

Under my method, if you are available, you can immediately pick up the call or let it go to voicemail. So my method saves the most time for the client and gives the best customer service. Return missed calls within one hour.

Eliminating barriers between you and your clients will breed a closeness and loyalty that will exceed that of your competition who haven't yet adopted this practice.

People, especially younger people, are used to instantaneous access to others. Traditional physical and social barriers and business standards have melted away, and most formalities related to business communication no longer exist.

Employing my methods will have your clients believing they are your only client.

16

Why Should I Hire You?

"Why should I hire you?" You should always be prepared to answer this question or the similar question: "Why should I buy your prodserv?"

Even if you have the best prodserv, you'll still need to include information about you and your Value Add—what you personally offer as part of the reason why a client should hire your firm or buy your product.

So how do I answer this question as a tax advisor and outsourced CFO?

My guarantees to you, my new client:

1) No one will care more about your family and business interests.
2) I will use my accumulated tax and business knowledge to enhance every aspect of your organization.
3) I will aggressively apply the tax law to gain every possible financial benefit and will customize strategies for tax minimization ongoing.

4) I will maintain your company's books and records and income tax returns in full compliance.
5) I will institute internal controls and policies that will maximize your profits and minimize the potential for fraud and embezzlement.

Then I ask: "When do I start?"

17

The Real Deal

We all know the phrase "the real deal" and know what it means when a colleague is referred to this way. I have also heard people say that "he or she brings it." We all know it when we see it. It can be an athlete, actor, teacher, boss, or rainmaker.

There are too many ways to describe what this is, but I strive every day to be it.

Whether it is a networking function with fifty other CPAs working the room, or a free consultation one-on-one with a new prospect, I want people to remember me for the right reasons. I want them to say: "Before I met Chris Whalen, CPA, I didn't know that so many skills could exist in one person, and I didn't know I needed all of them until now."

The advice in this book is meant to help you also become the most memorable.

Being "the real deal" and "bringing it" are what you want to strive for, especially in a homogeneous prodserv environment. You have to become the difference to the customer when your prodserv is perceived as a commodity.

Yes, your prodserv has to be the best, and you have to be able to prove that. If your prodserv is not the best in the industry, then look to move to a job at a company that has the best prodservs.

If you're not selling the best prodserv in your industry, you are already starting at a deficit and setting yourself up for failure.

No matter how stellar you are, and even if you are the real deal, a substandard prodserv will mean you will never reach your full income potential.

Along with your product, how are you presenting yourself? How are you being perceived in the marketplace? Study your competition. Go to networking functions and see what your counterparts are doing. How are they dressing? How did their promotional materials look? What are they doing to interact with clients in ways that you feel are successful that you can implement? What are they doing that's negative that you can capitalize on by differentiating yourself? In a homogeneous business environment, so much more relies on you and what you do and how you present yourself.

When I meet someone who is happy with their CPA, I always inquire as to why. What is my competition doing well with this person?

Bringing it never means being loud or seeking attention or monopolizing conversations. It means the opposite. I speak very little when I'm interacting with clients.

We have all seen loud buffoons who never gain respect and who are mocked once they leave the room.

I want to be understated, focused, and ready to implement strategies at all times, so I don't drink alcohol in business environments, but I buy plenty of drinks!

Try to fight the socialized pressure to drink. Even one drink will skew and diminish your thinking. Just one instance where someone sees you affected by alcohol, even slightly, will reduce their respect for you and confidence in your character.

Would you use a surgeon who you saw tipsy in the middle of the day? Or about to get in their car after happy hour after a few drinks? I wouldn't.

Business time is not social time. Social time is spent in your personal life. Of course there are social elements to business time, but don't confuse the two. Your reputation is in constant jeopardy during business time. The business grapevine can be worse for your reputation, even worse than the high school grapevine we all fondly remember.

Be jovial, funny, and intelligent, but dignified. Remember you are always selling on work time. Always be closing. Always be bringing it.

Everyday think of ways you can become the difference in the prodserv you are selling. Formulate and visualize the person you want the world to see. Find mentors who impress you and ask for their help and honest critiques.

People who bring it were just like you and me at one time. If they can craft an incredibly impactful persona, so can we. It takes a lifetime of daily practice, self-sacrifice, and hunger, and it is worth it.

Be deliberate about everything. Everything you do should come from analysis and forethought, not sudden impulses.

I would never say I personally am the real deal or that I bring anything. But I consciously and passionately strive for this every waking hour. Damn, sometimes I dream about bringing it, so I guess I strive for it during non-waking hours as well!

You will notice that people who are the real deal emotionally impact their audiences. They touch people deeply, almost like they have a way to understand thousands of people all at the same time. They are never preoccupied with themselves. Everything they do is purely an outward expression of their talent and love. Joy can almost always be seen in them as well.

The real deal is the smartest person in the room.

Those who bring it are contagious and extremely attractive on many levels.

No matter what you are selling, the more you touch people personally and envelope them in your confidence and ability to sympathize and empathize with them, the more you will be seen as the real deal.

The closing point to this chapter is if you sell a homogenous prodserv, YOU are the wild card in the potential sale. Your responsibility is enormous, and the pressure and scrutiny on you is immeasurable. If you don't make the right impressions, then you are also a homogeneous item, just like your prodserv. You will be a gallon of whole milk among millions.

18

You Must Be Your Own Brand

The most successful Homogenized Professionals become the most important part of their brands.

I cannot make it more clear than that. Not only are you striving to have clients use your prodserv over others, you want clients to request you specifically. You want referrals and potential new clients to demand you service their account.

In my world, my prodserv is secondary. People assume that I can perform the professional services I should be able to. So my brand is Chris Whalen, CPA, and the power of that brand goes well beyond the services I provide.

What do people expect from my brand? Prompt, professional, educated, and truly caring responses that seem to anticipate their questions. My clients expect me to understand their emotional motivations for what they're doing and not just the technical needs of the work they need done. You'll hear me talk about selling from the client, and that is one of the most important things I can do. I can do a hundred tax returns, and those client interactions will all be different.

A tax return is perceived as one of the most homogenized commodities! Of course this is untrue, but I have to battle that in my world every day! I can truly understand what this dynamic entails, no matter what you, the reader, are selling.

So I don't sell tax return preparation or consulting services. I sell Chris Whalen, CPA, tax return preparation and Chris Whalen, CPA, consulting services that people ask for by name.

19

If We Aren't Working for You, Then You Aren't Working at Your Best

You will see this saying at the top of my website. I try to live this every day and make it a reality. I tell people that yes, you are working as hard as you can, but you can't be 100% effective unless you hire my firm!

I think all Homogenized Professionals need to project this to their client base and make it a reality for them. No matter what prodserv you're selling, you have to instill this feeling within your clients. My clients understand that my value goes well beyond my homogeneous prodservs business consulting, and income tax preparation.

Remember you are the component that will bring your client's organization to 100% effectiveness. Without you, 100% effectiveness cannot be achieved!

I don't care if you are selling ping pong balls or toner cartridges or air filters.

If you are providing a prodserv that a commercial customer or an individual customer needs, then you have to understand the emotional basis and significance of that buying decision for that customer. No matter what you're selling, all customers have an emotional basis for buying decisions and for managing their companies and their operations.

Interview, study, and fully understand: 1) your clients' motivations and 2) their emotional and psychological goals. Every client is different, even when they are buying what seems to be the same generic product from you.

Motivations are usually driven by anxiety or mild fear.

This goes back to the chapter where I describe selling from the client (BTCM *Marketing* #8). All sales must start with objective selling from the client and understanding the client's modus operandi.

Once you learn these things, it becomes much easier to understand how exactly to communicate your value and in what ways the client needs you in order to reach their full potential.

If you aren't working for them, then they are not working at their best!

20

Dress Professionally, Not Provocatively

The more effective you are and the more true value you bring, the less your appearance matters. Don't let your appearance kill the sale before you open your mouth.

Present yourself in an understated, neat, well-groomed, yet professional way. Avoid fashion choices that will make you stand out when you walk into a room. Many people believe that standing out with fashion choices such as a bow tie or overly sexy dress are sales techniques. I have found this to never be the case. They are an unnecessary distraction.

This goes for men and for women. If you sexualize yourself while making your first impression, you will always be thought of as a sex object by those to whom you're trying. This is a terrible idea, as a sex object is never respected. This usually takes the form of over-emphasizing the physique. Today both men and women are using makeup, so my advice to both is to minimize the use of makeup and make it barely noticeable. It is possible to look very professional and not sexualize yourself.

Peacocking is only for peacocks.

Take the gender out of your selling. You never want to acknowledge the gender of your client for any reason, just as you never want them to equate you with your gender.

If you take this advice you'll be respected more and objectified less. Your sales will be much higher. Sexualizing yourself during selling is a very short-term strategy. Once you have presented yourself as a sex object, you can never backpedal. The prospect for getting respect and building a client relationship based on your business value alone may be lost forever.

This is especially good advice for those who are physically and facially attractive.

If you are one of them, no matter what clothes you wear or how little makeup you put on, you will be seen as a beautiful person. The excellent genes you inherited from your parents can actually work against you.

Most people believe an attractive appearance is an asset. At first, and for a quick sale, it might be.

Again, the more physically and facially attractive you are, the more this advice becomes important. Your looks can be an unnecessary distraction.

How can this be? How can good looks and sexualizing yourself be negative for someone?

Presenting yourself as a sex object can lead to frustration and a feeling of being teased by your clients. Increased sexual desire and attraction that doesn't become consummated leads to feelings of rejection and resentment. This is true in both men and women.

Before anyone feels I am preaching to women only, I come across just as many men in great shape, with form fitting shirts and trousers, who definitely stand out instantly for the wrong reasons. Before a word is spoken, the first impression they make is something that can't be taken back.

That is why it is so critical to understate your sexuality and your gender in professional environments. There's plenty of time after work to peacock. During the work day, in your office or on sales calls, is never the time.

Spend your time doing your homework, becoming the best at what you do, and also becoming indispensable to your clients and/or superiors. At the same time, purposefully understate your appearance. Strive to look neat but not to stand out for any physical or sexual reason.

This may sound counterintuitive, but my thirty years of business experience tells me that trying to physically stand out is a big mistake and can hurt your professional trajectory.

How do you know if you're dressing appropriately? In a group of people, do you simply blend in or do you instantly stand out? Is it apparent you are quickly noticed above all others based on the provocative level of your dress?

Are you being complimented more than your peers on your appearance?

Again, you want first and foremost to be known because of your talent and the value you bring. You want those things to be your first and lasting impressions. If you make a first impression based on sexuality, it may be the only thing you are remembered for.

When a company takes a downturn financially and needs to cut staff internally or reassess the outside professionals they pay, the most effective staff are kept regardless of how they look. The eye candy is quickly let go. We can always find new eye candy once we have the money in the budget again.

If you fear that changing your manner of dress will hurt your sales, I suggest you find a profession that values your abilities. Never make being a sex object a part of your selling success. It demeans and cheapens you.

21

The Greatest Show on Earth

Everyone likes a show, but be careful to not be cartoonish or clown-like when you're dealing with your clients. I have met many sales people and professionals who overdo things.

So what do I mean here in this chapter? I mean that people want to be entertained, and part of selling is having a personality and making people feel comfortable and happily engaged. You want to make them laugh, to make them feel important, understood, and cared for all at the same time.

Now, not everyone is a salesperson. Just because you're a business owner does not mean you're an entrepreneur. Just because you have the title of salesperson does not mean you can effectively sell anything.

When selling homogeneous prodservs, the personality of the seller is a key component to close deals. You may have the best prodservs, but if you can't convey that and sell your added value, the customers will never know it.

For example, there are many CPAs in the world, and all are my competition.

Many of them are technically excellent, but that is only 1% of creating an effective and successful CPA firm. They do have great skill, but they don't have the ability to communicate that to the marketplace, and so they languish in obscurity.

This is why your "show" is extremely important. It is your showmanship that will communicate all the great benefits you offer.

Yes, it is important to know your prodserv and to be able to communicate the details of those. But if all you're offering is a menu you are going to describe to potential customers, then you might be setting yourself up for failure. I get so many emails from colleagues that just give me a list of services they offer, similar to a menu. I tend to ignore these. Most people do.

Showmanship starts with knowing your audience. Remember that. You need to learn to convey your message to diverse groups of people at all times. If you have a canned presentation, it might only work for one-tenth of 1% of the population, understand?

Think about that. I always modify my presentations ahead of time. You will read in this book how I prepare for meetings so I won't go into that here. But true showmanship starts from the client—or in this case, creating your show or production starts from the client perspective.

This should be constant whether you are having a phone call with someone or setting up a presentation for five hundred people.

Knowing your prodservs must become like muscle memory to you, similar to what athletes experience. It is the showmanship portion where you adapt your presentation to specific selling situations that present your prodservs in the most palatable way to your customer audience.

Tell a great story, put on a great show, and offer the best prodservs—all at the same time, if possible—and your close rate will increase.

22

Your Internet Presence Is Your First Impression

Years ago, before the internet, first impressions were made face-to-face, usually in meetings in coffee shops or offices. Today many first impressions are made online and without you knowing about it.

I urge all of you to go online right now and put in your name and see what comes up. Objectively, does this look impressive to you? If not, it probably will not look impressive to your prospects. Then put in my name, Chris Whalen CPA, just those three words, and see if you feel that my internet presence and my first impression is substantial enough. I have worked very hard on this aspect of my marketing, and I feel it's one of the most important.

It is still true that you only get one chance to make a good first impression. Do all you can to make your internet presence as substantial as possible so it takes up multiple pages as mine does.

Perhaps you will notice when you do an online search for your name that one or two items are relevant, current, and relate to you. But other search results may be outdated and may not specifically relate to you. This is what you want to avoid.

There are several ways to increase your online presence. Many companies can help you with this. If a company says they do this for a living and can increase your ranking, ask them for five references. Be sure to call each one directly and also search for them on the internet to see what kind of work they do. It's very easy to see what someone is capable of.

I have much larger competition. They have marketing departments. However, I rank higher than them. When people search the web for CPA services, many times mine is the first firm they call.

You can achieve this as well. Learn about SEO. Learn how Google works with regard to rankings. Learn how to become a Google-verified business.

Use the advice in this book about posting original and solution-specific content and avoid posting generic material or the material of others.

23

Should I Automate My Communications for Follow-Ups?

I believe there is a benefit to automating some client interactions. For example, when an order is shipped, it can trigger an email with a client satisfaction survey. (More on this in BTCM *Client Specific* #61.) However, I like to control when more significant follow-ups are executed.

In BTCM *Technology* #76, I discuss how I use my calendar. One event type I have is the FU, or Follow-Up. Instead of having a programmed email or text scheduled to be sent on a certain day, I remind myself that one is due, and then I can decide if still want to send it. It is easy for a scheduled response to no longer be relevant. Your staff may have spoken to the client already, and then sending that scheduled item will make you look out of touch and confused. Or maybe the situation now warrants a phone call or onsite visit.

The business world is dynamic, and leaving scheduled canned responses in a queue somewhere would give me one more thing to worry about.

Fresh is always better than canned!

24

Do Not Send Emails or Texts on Holidays

Just don't.

There is never a need to send out holiday greetings to business contacts or clients. Although your sentiments may be genuine, these emails are quickly deleted along with other spam.

I have a significant position in a client's life, with personal connections, etc. And I would never send a personal email to a client, especially a generic one related to a holiday.

If you have already taken this advice, then you can skip the rest of this chapter. If not, read on.

On holidays and other national days off, I should get zero emails in my inbox!

People want to relax on days off, especially holidays. So please do not send out any emails or texts on those days. Period.

If you need to, compose emails and leave them in your draft folders and send them out at 9:00 am on the next workday.

Why should we give someone a non-critical email, especially on a holiday? Why would you want their new-email-notification-sound to go off when they are opening Christmas presents with their children?

This interrupts the truly important moments in life. It forces them to open an email, because in today's competitive world, people instantly have anxiety until they know the contents of every new message.

This comes down to respect, and I see this as part of the status update mentality so prevalent today. Who would honestly think that their email would be welcome on a holiday? A narcissist, most likely.

People are constantly tethered to work. They want to break that tether, especially on holidays, and we should allow them to.

I suggest you ask business contacts and clients, just as I do, to refrain from sending me non-work-related emails and to refrain from sending me emails on holidays and national days off completely. I promise them the same respect.

See BTCM *Marketing* #5, Only Share Specific and Original Content, for important information that relates to this chapter.

Mindset/ Philosophy/ Quality-of-Life Tools

25

Maintain Peace in Your Personal Space at All Costs

One key to commercial and business success is maintaining the most peaceful emotional space possible. There truly is no other way to reach your full potential.

You have every right to maintain peace in your personal space. And you should do that at all costs. There is nothing and no one that should ever be allowed to disrupt this space. You need to be mature enough to make personal changes for yourself and your family's future.

One way that I get to that peaceful personal space is through Transcendental Meditation®. I highly recommend that to everyone. It is one of my most important personal and business tools.

Many clients I consult with have business issues they need help working out. But I've never seen a business issue upset someone more than a personal issue. I often find that business issues are stemming from personal issues that are unresolved. In my consulting role, I have clients do a personal inventory, especially of close personal relationships. Once this is done, I sometimes find that clients need to make significant adjustments, which may include eliminating certain people from their personal space or modifying their interactions with specific people.

Take a moment and be honest and objective with yourself. Are any of your personal relationships causing you emotional upheaval and stress?

1. Spouse/Romantic Partner - Any NO answers? Move on asap.
    a. Do you have the same comfort level with them as when you are alone?
    b. Are they a source of nonjudgmental support and love at all times?
    c. Are they meeting your needs? Physical? Emotional? Spiritual?
    d. Do they respect you?
    e. Can you tell them everything on your mind without fear?

2. Siblings/Parents - Any NO Answers? Distance yourself asap.
    a. Are your parents fair and do they never play favorites?
    b. Do your siblings/parents keep your confidences?
    c. Do your siblings/parents show you the same amount of love, attention and concern that you show them?

d. Are your siblings/parents fully functioning adult people?
e. Do your siblings/parents communicate calmly and with respect at all times?

You have every right to confront the people in question and give them an ultimatum. Either their behavior and treatment of you changes, or they will lose the benefits of having you in their life for good.

We have all heard of doing a personal relationship inventory, but the one I developed goes beyond the norm. Yours should as well.

It's done in a workshop environment and, depending on the number of people in your personal circles, it may take a significant amount of time. One conversation cannot unearth where the underlying personal relationship issues are. Many of us are in dysfunctional relationships, but it is very hard for those within them to see the damage they are causing us. Getting a third party to help with this can bring clarity very quickly.

This one piece of advice and the detailed work I do to assist clients in this area is some of the most life-changing, emotion-modifying, and outlook-altering work I do.

I strongly urge you to engage in this type of work as soon as possible. If you do this honestly and objectively, and make relationship changes, the benefits can be exponential and lifelong. I promise you.

Is your personal life a calm blue ocean? Or are there tsunamis crashing into you every day?

26

Rushing Is Happiness's Arch Enemy (Time Management Is Happiness's Best Friend)

I have an engineer-level obsession with saving time. The more you take my advice, the more time you will save, and the less rushed you will feel. You may see a direct increase in happiness!

People are stressed more than ever. Over the past three decades I have seen an increase in anxiety among my clients. A large part of this is people feeling late, rushed, and that they're not going to make their deadlines. To put this in a simpler way, a large part of today's increased stress comes from a lack of time management. But this is in our control. That is the good news.

Now, if you are someone who does not like what you are doing, then there is really no way I can help you get to the next level. No one can. Do everyone a favor and find a career you can be passionate about.

But, if you really enjoy your work, I promise you can get to the point where stress levels are reduced and work satisfaction is increased.

Time management is the most important tool here.

You need to take some time and self-observe. That alone takes practice.

You need to dissect each anxiety-inducing work and life area.

I can hear you saying: "Chris! I don't have time to dissect anything right now!"

Ah, and therein lies the problem. There is no way you can be 100% productive while living moment to moment, filled with anxiety, feeling rushed and late.

If you eliminated these time related stressors, or at least reduced them a great deal, your productivity would improve and so would your quality of life.

So let's say there's a project that's due soon and you are feeling stressed and behind schedule. Is that a pattern? If so, you need to correct it. Do you consistently get to this point with every project? We need to go back to the planning stage and work our way forward to see how we got to this point. When did you start to feel behind? Did some other distraction or project delay your main one?

Plan to be ten minutes early to every meeting and ten minutes early to work.

When I worked for someone else, my base eight-hour day was 8:30 am to 4:30 pm. I loved being in the office before everyone else. And adjusting my eight-hour work day this way allowed me to save time in traffic going and coming.

Time management has to include having realistic discussions with the boss about deadlines of deliverables. You need to be honest during these discussions. If you are too afraid to contradict your boss's requested delivery dates even though they are unrealistic, then you should not be running projects.

All too often we are asked to multi-task and put fires out, taking our attention away from scheduled work. When this happens, and before you agree to have your attention diverted, discuss with your direct supervisor/client that the delivery date of your current main project will have to be moved further into the future. Let your supervisor make the decision as to where they want your time spent.

If you are a supervisor, you need to understand and apply this principle to those who work under you. Overloading your subordinates is poor business practice.

You need to manage expectations. If you don't, then you will wind up at the same place, stressed and anxious with deadlines looming you cannot meet.

Do you take extreme stress home? Your families don't deserve that.

You need to stop stress and anxiety from controlling you and your actions. There's never a time when you should let anything outside of you affect you emotionally, remember that. When this happens, you need to analyze why you're feeling this anxiety, why you feel rushed, and what you could have done differently.

I use this process every day. I take it as a personal science experiment.

If you are often overwhelmed with anxiety, please seek professional help to learn the tools you need to reclaim your life, peace, and happiness. Stress can lead to serious medical effects if not controlled.

Stress and anxiety may seem like vague specters that emerge out of nowhere, but they usually are not. They are evolved reactions to how we are living our lives that have been with us since the dawn of man. I believe most sources of stress are environmental. These fight-or-flight reactions protected the caveman, but instead of letting them ruin our day, we can learn to use them to our advantage.

If I can use these tools to improve my quality of life, you can too.

It starts with being deliberate and analyzing your work and personal lives and being honest about what is causing the problem. Then you can develop methods and institute changes to improve your life.

27

Nonjudgment and Objectivity Are Keys to Success

Just as it's a mistake to judge people we meet in our personal lives, it is just as dangerous to judge potential clients for any reason. This could be related to their politics, finances, their manner of dress, their religion, sexual orientation, or the color of their skin.

Practice getting mentally ready for openness and a true care for your clients' needs, and eliminate any judgment or preconception.

Objectivity means taking your own personal feelings, social filters, and defensiveness out of your discourse with clients. It also means being completely open for every new client interaction and selling from the client and their needs.

Very few people can do this effectively, and it is something you need to practice. You should never walk into an initial sales call believing you have the answer for a client need. You may not. You should use the sales call as a way to attempt to convince yourself and not just the potential client that you have the right answers.

So let the client, through discussion, educate you as to what they need from a business service perspective and, most importantly, what their emotional motivations are for their purchasing decision. The emotional basis and motivations are the most significant investigative work you need to do. Yes, you can sell someone something, but if you can sell to someone's emotions and their modus operandi, the retention of that client will be much longer, and the client's satisfaction will be maximized.

All of the items listed at the start of this chapter—politics, finances, manner of dress, religion, sexual orientation, and skin color—impact a client's mentality. The main point here is you are selling to people and not just meeting a business need.

People have diverse filters based on so many factors, some discussed above. Learn as much as you can about all of the variations within each of those categories so you can customize your selling at all times.

Selling to a female of Inuit descent should be different than selling to a male whose family first came to America on the Mayflower.

Do you truly have the right solutions? Again, you cannot know this until you objectively understand all of your potential client's needs.

With each new client meeting, I have to prove to myself, and then to the client, that my firm has the best solutions. This humble approach to sales will have you become your own best critic.

Become your client's strategic advocate and never be just selling them something.

If you can't get there, don't even attempt to service them, as your selfish motives will quickly become clear and result in failure.

28

Desperation Leads to Self-Compromise Leads to Enslavement

Desperate times **DON'T** call for desperate measures! Try to avoid starting any negotiation or sales pitch from a place of desperation.

If you are feeling desperate, still make the sales call or engage in a negotiation, but try to mask your weakness.

Any seasoned customer or vendor will smell your desperation a mile away and realize they have the upper hand in any negotiation you're about to start. This could be during a sale to a customer, a negotiation for a cross-referral relationship, or product pricing. As you will read at least a few times in this book, rehearsing can be a great tool. I still use this tool today, and I did my first deals as a teenager in 1981.

Whether it is true or not, seeming to come from a position of strength, expert knowledge, confidence, and sincerity will increase your success rate.

You must always sound confident and upbeat on the phone and in person. Again, rehearse! Especially if you are new to selling.

When you're desperate, you can't convey the true value of your prodserv. When you sell or negotiate from a position of desperation, you will never get a premium for what you are selling. You'll be lucky to close the deal at a discounted rate or possibly a loss.

And if desperation has led you to make a bad financial deal or sale, or to sign a long-term contract that is not maximized for your benefit, you may have compromised your organization.

Then you are technically enslaved for the duration of that contract or terms of that sale.

The lesson here is to not only eliminate the appearance of desperation in your selling, but truly eliminate it as a basis for your selling in reality.

Please read the title of this chapter until you fully understand it. Then apply it to your business and personal lives. This applies to romance as well.

Desperation Leads to Self-Compromise Leads to Enslavement.

29

Be a Straight Line and a Circle Simultaneously

For business and sales success, you must be two contradictory things at the same time.

The first thing you need to strive to be is a 100-ton molten comet hurtling through space with no obstruction, not even gravity, at the speed of light, in a straight line. To your clients you need to be all powerful, strong, true, and unstoppable.

Your competition will want to get out of your way, and your clients will want that energy working on their behalf. Your competition must see you this way. You must be a presence in your competition's lives, intimidating, awe-inspiring. You also must be a presence in your clients' lives constantly nurturing, protective, brilliant, indispensable, forceful, unwavering, and strong. You want your competition to be talking about you.

The second thing you must be simultaneously is a circle. You travel on that circle, slowly and methodically. You must be as reflective and objective as a philosopher, reviewing your every prior step (client interaction) for accuracy and effectiveness. You should be ever traveling along the arc of your professional circle, dissecting and analyzing your every prior action, and honing your skill sets for tomorrow's work. This part of you is the objective, self-observant student, questioning yourself more than even your superiors or clients might. This second thing that you need to be, the contemplative, objective philosophical one, feeds and hones the first thing you need to be, the glowing, molten sales force of nature, that the marketplace has no choice but to recognize.

30

Anticipate Setbacks and Negative Interactions

I start and end each day with Transcendental Meditation. When I am done, I calmly make mental lists of things that could go wrong in my personal and business lives that day.

I try to anticipate how those things can impact me negatively in scheduled meetings, projects that are due, and those delivered. I then formulate answers, sometimes multiple answers, for each. I go over them, almost like a rehearsal. I strive and hope for excellence and peace, but I know there are so many things out of my control that may try to ruin both.

Remember to customize your rehearsed responses based on the client's personality. So you may have delivered the same prodserv to five clients, but your approach to their potential concerns may be different.

I don't do this in a nervous or anxious way. I role play possible conversations with clients and staff, and review possible emails and phone calls. This process takes great objectivity, but if done correctly it can enhance your customer service and your processes. Most importantly, it prevents you from being emotionally shocked and upset when a conflict does happen. That is the most important benefit.

Anticipating negative things is much different than worrying or having anxiety.

This exercise is not based on fear, but a purposeful and deliberate thought process meant to help you be at the ready when problems surface. You want to be ready for every eventuality and remain calm and in control when fires break out. These moments are when you will build confidence and loyalty, or lose them.

There is no greater confidence builder for your staff and no greater allegiance builder with your customers than a level-headed and capable person addressing what they perceive to be emergencies, as if you have had forethought and knew this problem was going to happen exactly when it did. All without breaking a sweat or raising your voice.

That is what this daily exercise will do for you. Many people are afraid to anticipate negatives and obstacles. Those people make their problems worse by not planning for them.

If you start to use this lesson, you will quickly see the benefits that it brings you.

You can then teach it to your staff. You can turn something that causes you anxiety and that becomes a cloud above your head into a useful business tool that enhances the peace and control you have over your entire life.

Problems will have to worry about you from now on, and not vice versa.

31

Burnout Is Real; Take a Break (or Two)

Constantly serving others is emotionally and physically draining. It is very easy to grow to resent your clients, spouse, children, and even your pets. They can sense your emotional state. Don't ever believe you can mask this. You cannot.

Taking time away from your work responsibilities and removing the tether of your phone and computers is very important psychologically and emotionally. It proves to your subconscious mind that you are not enslaved.

I don't just mean on the weekends. Every day there should be breaks where you are out of reach of your work responsibilities. This can simply be ten-minute periods where you leave your phone at your desk and take a brisk walk. I'm not talking about your lunch break; that does not count here. You definitely should take a full lunch break every day.

Taking a few minutes in the morning and in the afternoon for complete solitude, let's say to nap, daydream, meditate, or study the clouds in the distance, reclaims your emotional and psychological human space. This has been proven to lead to productivity gains and a much happier and longer life.

If you do this, you will be happier, and your work and life perspectives will improve.

Transcendental Meditation is one of my most important business and personal tools. I started using it in the mid-'90s, and it continues to enhance my life in ways I have never imagined. I meditate at least twice per day.

So take at least two **reclaiming-your-personal-space** breaks during your day besides lunch.

What does this do for you psychologically? Many of us suffer from separation anxiety if our phone is not on our person or if it is turned off. This reduces us to being slaves to our phones.

Wouldn't you like to reclaim your feeling of adult control and independence and start to live like a confident adult?

This enslavement problem calls for a form of cognitive behavior therapy. We consciously know that nothing terrible will happen if our phone is turned off or out of our sight for ten minutes, yet the thought of that happening can bring on an anxiety attack.

I hate allowing inanimate objects to control my emotional system. I personally take my own advice every day here. Even after a decade of doing this twice each day, I still have a visceral pang of fear in my belly sometimes the moment I turn that phone off and start meditating or taking a walk.

But when I turn that phone back on and realize the world has not ended, it elevates my emotional state and sense of confidence, and gives me some true freedom back. This brings my emotional system to a much calmer place and takes it out of the fight-or-flight mode we are all living in constantly today.

Curing burnout takes time, but it can be done. I consider these brief interludes carefree vacations that I get to look forward to twice each day instead of dreaming of a week off six months from now.

Send me a postcard!

32

The Power of Pausing

Business "flash fires" can ignite without warning. Many times, due to evolution, our emotional and psychological reactions to these "fires" can be much too extreme and damaging. Business problems are not predators trying to make a meal of us. They are just wrinkles in a dress shirt that need to be ironed out.

It is very important that we learn to do something we didn't evolve to do when faced with sudden emergencies. And that is to . . .

Pause.

Pausing is one of the most powerful tools we have. Pausing leads to contemplation, which leads to measured and deliberate responses. Pausing helps minimize your defensive reactions when it seems you are being attacked.

As an entrepreneur or team leader, your demeanor is the emotional barometer of your team. As you go, so goes the team.

This is especially important during times of business stress. When problems surface, your demeanor can make or break client and employee relationships. It is so easy during times of crisis for confidence to be lost in you and never regained.

Realizing this, I make this a focus and main part of how I handle crises. This is more important than fixing the problem, because, of course, it is assumed The Chocolate Milk can always fix the problem.

So I pause, and I don't race to put out the fire. The first step is to pacify those around me. Knowing their evolution-based reactions may be triggering their fight-or-flight responses, I make sure to exhibit a calm, relaxed, and confident demeanor. I want to bring everyone down to my rational emotional level before taking one step to fix the problem confronting us.

Once we have ALL paused collectively (and realize we are not about to become a predator's lunch), trouble-shooting can begin, and then solutions implemented.

Now, my entire team has their emotional and intellectual systems ready to work on fixing the problem, and not preoccupied with irrational evolution-based fears.

Why is this important? Our main jobs are not selling prodservs. Our main jobs are fulfilling the emotional needs of our clients and staff. The sooner we realize that, the more successful we will become.

Problems will arise daily, so concentrate on how those moments are handled and eliminate worrying about them. In the long run, the specifics of daily problems are forgotten. But your demeanor will never be. I use times of crisis as selling moments. Moments to sell myself as a leader, problem solver, and pacifier.

You will hear me say time and time again, client problems and complaints are the best time to increase your client's satisfaction and retention. An increase in a client's emotional state, although it may seem negative towards you during a crisis, is the place you want to insert yourself with solutions and emotional pacification as soon as possible. The quicker your response, the greater emotional payoff for the client and the greater potential future financial payoff for you.

The fact that I do accurate tax returns in my CPA practice is irrelevant. Accuracy is assumed and expected at a minimum. I need to serve and pacify other client needs in order to become The Chocolate Milk. Most of those other needs are emotional and psychological.

Providing the best prodservs, while filtering our work through a full emotional and psychological understanding of our clients, will lead to industry-leading success.

Using the Power of Pausing at times of crisis directly serves our teams' and clients' emotional and psychological needs. This increases their respect for us, their loyalty to us, and therefore client and employee retention. An increase in profits follows naturally.

33

Only Fight to Win When it Serves Your Purpose

Sometimes we expend energy and resources on winning an argument when the only benefit is the emotional payoff. This is a complete waste of time.

This can also be written as "only strive to win when it serves a tangible purpose." Losing is a valid course of action when winning gains nothing.

Proving that you are right about something should not be paramount, unless it furthers your goals and aims.

If it doesn't further your goals, do not spend the time proving that someone is wrong or that you are correct about anything.

The ego plays a huge role here. When faced with someone who has blatantly incorrect information, many of us have a hard time not attempting to correct them.

The mature person never allows any external force to impact their emotional system. This is the key to my daily happiness. The above is a great example of an external force doing just that. You want to be constantly self-observing and notice when this happens to you, and then work on eliminating it as soon as possible.

Removing these triggers can take some time, as they have been ingrained in many of us for decades. But your old way of thinking is now over, and a new, self-observant, objective you has arrived.

Back to this chapter's topic. If you find yourself having the emotional (insecure) need to correct someone, but with no business advantage at all, take time to pause and control yourself and move on to another task.

When you feel the need to defend yourself, this usually means you feel the need to answer to someone else. There are very few people you need to answer to.

Once you have gained insight and self-control in this area, you will then see that losing an argument, or losing at anything, can be just as satisfying as winning. Letting someone believe falsehoods about you can make your day.

In these situations you have won, as you didn't allow your insecurities to waste your time.

Again, remember, there are very few people to whom you need to answer. Live that last sentence consciously every day. I have since I was thirteen years old.

34

Be Realistic

This chapter could also be called "Manage Your Own Expectations."

Aim high, of course! But it can be emotionally dangerous to have unchecked and unrealistic expectations in any area of your life. In business, it can be financially costly as well. Your mind is an extremely hopeful and biased place! Learn to detach from it and objectively observe what you're doing and what you are planning.

How do I do this? I imagine another person presenting me with what I am planning. Just as I do in my selling, I evaluate my plan as if it was theirs.

This mental trick increases your objectivity and decreases your biases.

I use this method all the time, for both personal and business decisions.

For example, are you trying to assess if you should end a romance? Pretend your best friend is across the desk from you describing your situation as if it were theirs. Whatever advice you would give them, take yourself.

Don't treat your ideas and plans as a romantic interest you want to make happy, but as a complete stranger trying to convince you to do something.

In my consulting work, I often see people in management who have unrealistic expectations of their staff. You need to be realistic about your employees and what their capabilities are.

Many of these problems start during the interview process. Interviewing is an art that is falling by the wayside. We hear so much today about the automation of everything, and human resource services is becoming a victim. This is a tremendous mistake.

Doesn't that sound odd to you? Taking the humanity out of human resources? Of course it does. It would be like taking the cream out of ice cream. A bowl of only ice doesn't sound too appetizing.

What job skills are needed for open positions? If the job is full-time, or a traditional forty hours per week, then how much work should the right candidate be able to accomplish? Do you even know? What is your estimate based on? Have you thoroughly discussed this with the candidate as part of the interview process?

Before filling a position, you owe it to yourself and the candidate to fully understand the requirements.

Employees should have a clear understanding of what is expected of them prior to accepting a job. It is your responsibility to manage expectations here. The more clear you are, the more successful your hiring decisions will be.

Problems you are having with your employees might stem from inefficient hiring processes. If you hire the right person with the correct skills, and they fully understand their job duties and responsibilities, then they will be able to get the correct amount of work done within the time allotted.

If you find this is not the case, then you have made a bad hiring decision. Don't spend your time engaged in productivity-related friction with your staff. Realize this is your fault, and fire staff that are not performing.

Now, you can make educated hiring decisions so that staff members will be able to get the correct amount of work done during their forty-hour workweek. A new hire may require more money than the employee being replaced, but they will be worth it.

I want you to have grand and expansive visions for your future. But I want you to temper them with unbiased analysis and reasoning.

35

Don't Be Married to Any Idea, Especially Yours!

You and your ideas need to sign a prenuptial agreement! You should be in a constant state of questioning your decisions and your thought processes. You need to be your constant and greatest critic. Very often when we feel we have found the right answer to something, we are quick to share it. This can be a mistake. This is akin to popping the question too quickly! Like right after the first date! Feeling we have the right answer is simply the very first step in thousands that need to be taken before we can expose our proposed solutions. You want to test, test, and retest everything.

Put your solution through every possible permutation. Give your staff time to mull over new ideas, but don't put them on the spot to critique anything immediately, if you can help it. Allow them to work through possible scenarios as if your new idea were to be implemented.

You most likely have a varied client base; make sure you test it on average and usual clients, but also on those on the fringes. All the while make sure they know you are expecting feedback. Sometimes our ideas can be like a bad marriage—we're afraid to ask for feedback, we live with worry and fear of what our partner is truly thinking, and we have no idea of what our partner truly wants!

That is a recipe for unhappiness and divorce.

There is nothing more important than getting client feedback, especially when you are testing new ideas.

It is very easy to get defensive when hearing feedback, but that is an immaturity you cannot afford. I have seen many entrepreneurs fail because of their emotional frailty. The best entrepreneurs are open to objective and honest advice from all corners. This includes employees, clients, and family. Quite often it can include colleagues in the same or different industries. I look for feedback from all of these areas constantly. This keeps me up-to-date on the emotional business landscape, and it keeps me humble to realize that all of my ideas are not perfect.

Remember, the narcissistic entrepreneur is not an entrepreneur for long.

So should you be married to your ideas? NO! Marriage requires a long-term commitment. Your ideas should only get your commitment when they have proven their loyalty and value to you and only as long as they serve your business objectives fully. Once they do not, discard them like a bad first date.

36

Never Speed Towards a Red Light!

It always amazes me when I see cars approaching a red light but I don't see brake lights until the very last moment when they need to stop. Sometimes it seems like they're still accelerating even though the light is obviously red.

This is a great analogy for how business owners approach their business. Very often we are given clear signs that we won't be able to continue past a certain point. But just like a speeding car, we don't hit the brakes soon enough.

Imagine that we compare our businesses to that speeding car. Let's think of the types of damage we are doing to our vehicle as we approach stoplights. We are breaking very hard, which stresses brakes, shock absorbers, and the frame. It dramatically stresses the transmission as well.

Imagine for a second, that we take a different approach as we approach the red light. From the distance we see the red light, and we immediately take our foot off the gas pedal.

This allows us to coast, expending no energy and putting no stress on our components.

This gives us time to think and strategize. Do we want to get to the red light? Is there traffic ahead? Is there a turn we can use to avoid that light? How long will that red light take to turn back to green? Coasting for a moment gives us extra time and therefore more options than we had before.

The same applies to business. You want to give yourself as much time to pause as possible. This gives you options, and it protects your organization's chassis. You are going to come across many red lights in business every day. Take some time in the next few days and try to spot them. Make mental notes of where they are and how they appear, and then make it a point to approach them differently than you currently do.

Many of us are flooring it every day, all day. We rarely take time to coast, take a breath, and look around. We may be missing many options, many alternate routes, many beautiful overlooks that we never saw before where we can park for a moment and meditate over a beautiful landscape.

So make it a point to always pause the minute you see a red light ahead of you.

To take that a step further, imagine every green light you see can turn red in an instant. Have you planned for that eventuality?

No good can come from accelerating towards a red light and slamming on your brakes when you get to it.

37

GO TO SLEEP!

Sleep is the most important business tool. Bar none. You need eight hours of sleep, not just eight hours in bed, every night.

Make sure to turn off all electronics and anything else that may overstimulate your eyes an hour before bedtime. I usually meditate ninety minutes before going to bed. I may read in that last hour before bed, but something physical, not digital, and always a book or article that has nothing to do with work. I am a big historical nonfiction reader. Listening to audiobooks in complete darkness is a great way to get your entire being ready for sleep.

I meditate as soon as I wake up in the morning. During sleep, our brains work overtime while healing the rest of our body. Upon waking, our brain may be more stressed than before falling asleep the night before.

Meditation heals our brain by allowing it to rest. Think of this as a system's check of your brain's electrical and chemical systems. You'll be shocked at how great you feel all day when you can start the day with your brain's electricity and chemistry at womb-like levels.

38

Budget for Quality of Life (Living to Work Is No Life at All)

This chapter is self-explanatory. I urge all of my clients and employees to budget for quality of life as well as financial savings.

I am never thinking of a future time when I'm going to enjoy myself and finally relax, say in retirement. I enjoy myself consciously every single day in many ways. This can mean taking a full weekday off, or playing hooky for an hour and a half from work to go to a bookstore, or meditating at lunch time.

Every day we all have time to budget for. Make sure some of those twenty-four hours are carved out with specific activities that enhance your quality of life.

I try to have the attitude that my work is incidental. It provides the financing to take care of and enjoy myself every day.

Try to have the mental state that you're permanently on vacation, but some days you need to check in to work.

Instead of having days with no planned personal enjoyment, try to break up the day in the opposite way.

Every day I make sure I prioritize and schedule things for myself, some kind of luxury and something totally unnecessary for my work life. Doing this every day and not simply waiting for a weekend or a vacation is so critically important for my mental health and happiness.

Make your work simply small interruptions of your constant enjoyment of life. Take the time now to look at your calendar for the next week. Actually schedule things for yourself, and do that every week from now on.

39

Your Measure of Success Should Only Come from Within

Subtitle: Never Let Anything Outside of You Impact Your Emotions Negatively

This comes from my following of Taoist & Buddhist philosophies. For a week or two, I would like you to make a note of any negative emotions you feel and how many of them are coming from something outside of yourself.

Your spouse, your coworkers, your boss, your children? Are they bringing about negative feelings inside of you? If so, make it a priority to eliminate those reactions as soon as possible. Now, I didn't say eliminate THE PEOPLE, but only their ability to impact your emotions negatively.

Most of us are allowing external things too much control over our emotional systems, and that is insane. How can we ever expect to be happy or feel satisfied when our feelings of satisfaction, self-esteem, and self-worth are totally out of our control?

I hope you're saying that is a good question, because it is.

When I'm deep in meditation, I use visualization to change my emotional reactions to these triggers. For example, let's say that when I see a certain client's face come up on my phone when they are calling me, it turns my stomach with anxiety. I can use visualization deep within meditation to change that emotional reaction.

I cannot more strongly urge you to self-observe from now on. Objectively study your emotional and psychological reactions. Identify things or people that impact your emotions negatively and then work to undo their ability to hurt you. I suggest using a journal at first when you begin this process. And there is no shame in seeking a therapist's help here. Once we have revelations and are truly conscious for the first time, it can be overwhelming.

You will be much happier. My personal satisfaction stems from putting forth my best effort and being a good Christian person every day. I cannot worry about popularity, the satisfaction of others with my performance, or the outcomes of my efforts. Don't be a slave to results or popularity.

Imagine living a life where it does not matter if others approve of you or what your results are. Imagine being content only putting forth your best effort and knowing you will not achieve success all the time.

All we can do is try our best, and that is all we should expect from ourselves. More importantly, those in our lives should expect nothing more from us.

Even if I fail a hundred times in a day, and the people around me are upset and annoyed at me, I sleep like a baby knowing that no one has tried harder than me.

Your definition of success must go well beyond the closing of the next deal.

Attaining financial success should only be one of the means to your end and not your life's meaning. That end is happiness and peace in your personal space. I have had business highs and lows, but I don't let either impact my overall happiness and feeling of satisfaction about life.

Our level of effort and commitment for those we love, and how we translate those into actions, should be the measure of our success every day, not the results from that effort.

So take some time now and analyze how you are gauging your self-worth and personal success. If these things are linked to your financial success, then you are leaving your self-worth and life satisfaction in the hands of things outside of yourself. As you get to know me and read more about my philosophy, you'll see that is one of the biggest mistakes you can make.

So from now on, self-observe and see where your feelings of satisfaction and dissatisfaction are coming from. Are they coming from inside of you? That is where they should be coming from. Are your happiness and feelings of personal satisfaction coming from things? I call these External Definers, and you need to eliminate their impact on your emotional state.

People in our lives are also External Definers. Are you overly concerned with what people in your life feel about you? Is your romantic partner's approval something that weighs heavily on your self-worth? Do you care too much what your coworkers feel about you? Do you have a very high level of need to be liked? Are you unable to express yourself to certain people in your personal life? That should be seen as an emergency, and it must be changed immediately. No adult should be afraid to express themselves to another adult. Any relationship you are experiencing this within is not a healthy one for you, and most likely it never will be. Do the hard but mature thing: confront the other party with your honest self and feelings and let the cards fall where they may. If you remain silenced, you are a slave.

These are significant weaknesses that stifle your ability to become a fully functioning adult person. These leave you in an infantile position figuratively wanting the approval of parents. From now on be honest with yourself as to how significant other people's feelings are about you and how they are impacting your actions.

Too often I see disingenuous people maintaining perceptions of others and never exposing their true selves. For example, maybe you want your mother to believe you are a certain person. You want your romantic partner also to believe you are a different person, and you want your boss and coworkers to believe you're someone else. This is no way for an adult to live. Imagine all of the time and energy wasted.

You need to become the person you want to be and let the world see that person regardless of the fallout. This is true confidence and true maturity.

At work, though, is not the place to fully reveal your personal self at any time. That is not necessary.

Far too often people share too much detail of their personal life in the office. I think this is a mistake. I believe you should be cordial with your coworkers, as well as cooperative and helpful. That does not mean telling your life story every day. It is so easy for you to become a burden and also a laughing stock when you are not around. Don't mistake people's politeness and patience for friendship. Very few coworkers will become personal friends. The more you reveal personally, the more vulnerable your job becomes.

The more personal information you share, the more ammunition you provide potential enemies you work alongside.

Your coworkers have enough work to do and their own personal problems. Do not burden them with more from you.

This topic focused more on the personal than business, because I believe that until we are fully happy and functional in our personal lives, we cannot achieve our full business and professional potential.

40

If You Don't Like Your Prodserv, I Cannot Help You

If you don't truly love what you are doing to earn a living, then change careers as soon as possible.

I have worked with thousands of clients, and I have learned to never take on one who is dispassionate about his or her work. There is no way to achieve your full business potential if you are not genuinely fulfilled by your daily work.

I love everything about my business: even my mailbox, paper clips, business cards, and outdoor sign.

Your day cannot be filled with constant excitement and success, but every moment, even the most mundane, should be thought of as necessary and exciting components of this vocation you chose for yourself.

Everyone is different, and not all jobs can bring personal satisfaction to all people.

Don't think it is some deficiency within you if you are not happy. I have met doctors who realized medicine was not their calling the day after their residency ended.

There is no crime in exploring different disciplines. Find one that evokes passion within you. You owe it to yourself and your loved ones.

Someone who is not fulfilled in their work can be unbearable to deal with in and out of the office.

If you are in that position, no matter how much you offer to pay me, I cannot help you live up to your business potential.

The old adage says it best: "Like what you do, and you will never work a day in your life."

41

Be Utilitarian and Minimalist

All too often business owners or sales reps believe they can impress with glitz or excessive information. This could be an ostentatious office or automobile, or extravagant presents or entertainment outings. It could mean voluminous and flashy marketing materials that few people will ever read.

Often this means dressing provocatively, which is one of the worst mistakes you can make. Dress neatly and conservatively, and be well groomed.

Make sure your car is clean inside and out, as you never know when you will need to drive a client somewhere. A neatly kept Japanese economy car is more impressive than a German luxury car filled with wrappers, old coffee cups, and a backseat filled with who knows what. People mostly notice when thing are dirty, not when they are clean and neat. My clients don't care what car I drive.

Become an expert about your prodserv and a student of your potential clients and the marketplace. If you do these things well, the pretty office, luxury car, and other window dressing will not be important.

What does utilitarian mean? It means something is designed to be useful or practical rather than attractive. I want to be thought of as utilitarian first and foremost, although from certain angles, I can't help but be attractive. ;) Evaluate things and people based on their utility above all else.

What is a minimalist? Someone who strips things down to their essential and necessary elements is a minimalist. Eliminate unnecessary layers that don't add to the finished prodserv.

Just the facts, Ma'am.

42

Troubles, Anxieties, and Self-Doubt Are Sticky Notes

I use meditation and visualization as a tool to work on emotional obstacles, especially anxiety.

Many of us wake up in a high state of tension. Then this tension level escalates to intolerable and unhealthy levels as the morning progresses. By lunchtime many of us are physically and emotionally exhausted, severely decreasing our productivity and quality of life.

That is why I meditate, especially first thing in the morning. My main goal when I start my day is to get my brain and my emotional system into an almost womb-like state. I want to start the day at a negative level of tension if that's possible, so during the day, although tensions will escalate, they'll never get to an intolerable level for me.

Many westerners don't truly understand meditation. Now, I'm not an expert on this, of course, but I want to tell you exactly how it helps me emotionally and physiologically.

I also gain great spiritual benefits but those are not important in this discussion.

Let's imagine that you've had a perfect night's sleep. The best sleep ever. What happens during sleep? Well, your whole body gets to rest and it gets to heal itself.

But what many people don't realize is that the brain is working overtime during your sleep. Especially during a good sleep session, your brain can be exhausted by the time you wake up. So meditation is the time when you allow your brain to heal. During meditation the electricity in your brain will normalize and become a very low hum, which also gives your brain the time to check its levels of hormones such as serotonin and dopamine.

I hope you see the benefits of starting each day like this. Imagine you could start every day with your brain's electricity and chemistry at its most calm and regulated state.

I also meditate for twenty minutes one or two hours before bed. This sets up a perfect cycle where I am as calm as possible, emotionally and physically, prior to going to sleep. It allows my sleep to be incredibly deep, restful, and recuperative. Then I wake up the next day and meditate, assuring that I, not the world, will be in control of my emotions.

I call this my "Cycle of Calmness," and I highly recommend it!

My sleep patterns and my associated meditation regimen are the most important things I use to maintain my personal happiness and business success.

So why did I mention sticky notes in the title of this chapter?

During meditation, I have learned to visualize things that trigger me, and to modify my reactions to them.

Many of us have triggers that cause a negative reaction in our emotional systems.

I am constantly vigilant to make sure that nothing outside of me impacts my emotional system in a negative way. But of course I'm human, and some things do bother me. This is one of the reasons I use visualization within my meditation sessions.

It works like this. When you're in a calm and meditative state, you can bring that trigger into your mind and emotional space. Then you can work on applying a different reaction to it.

Many people don't realize that these strong emotional reactions are as flimsy as sticky notes. You can learn to peel them off of your heart and soul and throw them away. Visualization during meditation will facilitate this.

You can learn to never be impacted by triggers again. My daily emotional mission is to never allow anything or anyone outside of me to negatively impact my emotional system.

Purposefully making yourself more calm and unaffected by the outside world can do wonders for anxiety as well. If you start and end your day at your most serene, calm, and happy, all of the triggers you encounter will impact you much less.

43

Competition Creates Individual Excellence, Unique Identities, and Functioning Adults

Competition is one of the most important things for human beings. It is the best way to bring out excellence in people and helps form a true identity. It also forces everyone to decide where to put their energy.

For example, recently in the news there have been cheerleading squads that are accepting everyone who wants to participate in the squad. This is extremely damaging for all parties. It diminishes the work and effort of those who wanted to try out and truly compete for a position. It also now allows people to be on the squad whose only qualification is an interest! To allow participation based only on interest is the path to mediocrity. Now this squad will never be able to compete with other squads who base acceptance on merit.

Those who wanted to simply participate and are allowed to are also done a tremendous disservice. They should be taught to find something they are passionate about and strive for excellence.

In these cases there is usually an exodus from the activity of the competitive and passionate people, leaving mainly a social group, and a cheerleading squad in name only.

Although it might seem we are protecting people's feelings when everyone wins an award or everyone has a chance at bat, in the long run it stunts their development as human beings and leads to perpetual immaturity and entitlement.

Just imagine if Steve Jobs and Bill Gates grew up in a time where everybody played t-ball, and there weren't any tryouts for sports. Today parents force their kids to be on a team, even when the kids aren't interested and they don't have the ability or skill. If Bill Gates and Steve Jobs didn't have to face rejection, it would have stunted their growth as human beings. And we never would have had Apple computer and Microsoft had these two geniuses not been able to pursue their passions and real interest.

Participation must be based on the true urgency that people show for that particular activity.

This is how people become The Chocolate Milk in life. If there is no competition, especially for children, then what we have is a group of youngsters who will have interest in fewer activities than prior generations. Think about it: if there are no tryouts for baseball, and the parents are very interested in their kids playing baseball, then that's what the kids will do.

So this becomes a vicarious status event for the parents, which is a subject for another book.

We need to get back to a time when merit was key. Remember merit comes from effort, enthusiasm, passion, and the pursuit of excellence. Merit does not exclude anybody; it gives the individual credit and award for all the hard work they've done. Isn't this the kind of thing we want to perpetuate in society? This is how I was raised. Everything had to be earned, whether it was getting on a sports team or dealing with the group of kids in the alley in Queens where I grew up.

I was constantly forced to make a decision as to where I wanted to put my energy and what my goals were. Today society tells us what our goals are, and that is extremely dangerous. Today equality of outcomes is being championed above the recognition of merit.

I believe this has created generations of children and now young adults who don't have a true individual identity or a true unique character. They are looking for validation outside of themselves, which is the ultimate weakness.

Many of them are having a hard time finding their place in society. This is especially true of young men. I have been dealing with human resources issues and the hiring of college graduates since 1990.

And every year that has gone by since then, I have seen maturity into adulthood delayed more and more. Years ago many people graduated from college in four years and were expected to have a full-time job in their major right after school. Today graduating in four years is becoming less frequent, and graduates living on their own has also been extremely delayed. It seems like the graduates of today are about six to eight years behind the graduates of 1990. And again, I stress this about boys and men more than women.

But sorry to digress into a societal analysis. All of this applies to the workplace. All of the same dynamics are at play in the workplace.

You need to discover where your employees' passions lie. So maybe everyone doesn't get a bonus, or only the best salesperson gets a shot at making commission off of the latest prospect.

Not everyone deserves the "Glengarry Leads."

Can you imagine if business was run the same way participation-based societies run? That would mean you would have to give everyone the same chance to do the same work regardless of their capacity and ability.

Now of course you know that would be a disaster for your organization, but why doesn't everyone realize that doing the same thing is a disaster for society? There is no difference. It hurts everyone and everything.

Most importantly, it hurts the individuals. Allowing them to participate in anything they wish is destructive and regressive. Open participation on a whim, without requiring hard work, and most importantly the possibility of rejection, has been the norm for a few decades now, and the impact is far reaching. Our children are weaker in all areas: physically, emotionally, and psychologically.

Rejection, failure, and sometimes even being bullied are the most important life experiences that lead to a fully functioning adulthood. If you're not allowed to fail, are never rejected, and never have to learn to navigate around a bully, then your development can be severely retarded.

44

Never Pick Up a Hitchhiker Who's Not Walking

My grandfather taught me this saying.

I was born in Queens, New York, and spent the first part of my life there. My maternal grandfather owned a fruit and vegetable business. He had a large walk-in truck he would use for his deliveries, and when we were not in school, my brothers and I would go out with him on deliveries. This was my first exposure to an entrepreneur, and the lessons I learned at his side still guide me today. He is the person who taught me the Imperato Doctrine explained in BTCM *Marketing* #8. Make sure to read and understand it.

Back in the 1970s, hitchhiking was much more common than it is today. Sometimes, driving in the truck, we would see someone standing on the side of the road with their thumb out but not walking toward their destination.

My grandfather would say, "Boys, never pick up a hitchhiker who's not walking. If they aren't in a rush to get where they're going, why would I stop and help them? Now, if you see someone running down the street with their thumb up, that is the person you might want to pick up, because they are doing all that they can to get where they're going."

As I grew up I realized this is a fantastic metaphor, and he was teaching us a life lesson about human nature, not just hitchhikers. In my life, I am always on the lookout for anyone figuratively hitchhiking but not walking.

What does this mean? This simply means there are people that expect others to do their heavy lifting while they expend minimal personal energy themselves. These are people to avoid in all areas of your life, not just in business.

Now, I am not talking about clients here, as they hire you to pick them up while they are hitchhiking, even when they are not walking. I earned countless fees this way!

Personally and professionally, surround yourself with industrious people who take pride in their ability to take care of themselves and who want to participate fully in their lives and yours. Align yourself with people who take pride in their personal contributions to their endeavors.

In my CPA practice, I work with many partnerships, and all too often I see a great disparity in the enthusiasm, effort, and acumen between the partners. It is so apparent when someone is doing the majority of the work, and someone else is taking advantage.

One of the main reasons why I am a sole practitioner is that my success rises and falls on my effort, and it is difficult to find someone who will be as passionate and committed as I am to the success of my enterprise.

So how does this apply in business? Well, you should apply this rule to employees you hire as well as subcontractors you partner with. Hard workers who bring a lot of value can attract hitchhikers who are not walking.

I want you to be extremely observant about this.

It is very easy to become a babysitter for others in our personal and business lives. Again, I am not talking about clients here, as we are supposed to coddle, nurture, and pacify them in every way possible. But the more you get rid of people who are not pulling their weight, the less work that will be for you.

I tell everyone I have enough work of my own to do, and if you can't do your own work and need me to step in too often, then you become a liability for me and you'll need to be removed from my professional life. In essence, these people are taking money out of my pocket. The time I'm spending doing someone else's job is time I cannot bill my client for. No need for me to explain why that is a problem.

Sometimes, we keep these people in our lives without realizing it. But not any longer.

This weakness actually comes from a good place of wanting to nurture others. But except for our role as parents, it does everyone a disservice if we maintain these types of relationships. It keeps the other person professionally stunted and does not allow them to grow into a fully functioning adult person.

Do your best to hold everyone accountable to what their responsibilities are. If you manage people, you need to delineate and explain clearly what those responsibilities are. Make sure there is follow-through and there are regular performance reviews.

Be a mentor, though, not a dictator. All professional guidance should be expressed in a nonjudgmental way with a respectful tone. The values and skills you're looking to instill should only edify and never disparage.

Let's say after reading this you do an inventory of your relationships and discover some of these immobile hitchhikers. You have no choice now but to approach them and discuss changes that need to be made.

As you can imagine, this confrontation can create a lot of friction. They have come to overly depend on you and may get angry and frightened. But this is where you need to be strong and not fall for tears or shaming language.

People have to earn the benefits of a relationship with you. They need to be working to the greatest of their ability to better themselves and your organization. In personal relationships, the rules are the same. People need to stop taking value from you and start bringing it, or they will be removed from your life.

If you choose to keep someone in your life who takes value from you and doesn't give it, that is a weakness you may need professional help to overcome. Consciously maintaining someone's dependence on you can be thought of as cruel, although some people would believe you're simply being a Good Samaritan.

45

The Truth Usually Lies Somewhere in the Middle

I try not to take things at face value. Most people tell their version of the truth, but sometimes emotions can alter their recollections.

This can happen when people are upset or are desperate about something. So when dealing with staff members or clients, we sometimes have to do some detective work to find the factual truth.

When does this come into play?

1. Client calls you to complain about how your staff treated them.
2. Employee feels he is being bullied by coworkers.
3. Client says you have not delivered per your engagement letter or contract.
4. Staff member calls out sick.
5. Staff member feels their workload is too heavy.

6. Client gets an IRS notice, and they are sure agents are on their way.
7. Staff member claims they have left numerous unanswered voicemails and emails to a client assigned to them.

The best advice is to not get reigned in emotionally in any case. Remain impartial and guide all parties to a collective remedy that respects everyone.

Observe yourself and suppress any defensiveness that will naturally want to surface. It is so easy to feel personally attacked.

Whether you are a business owner or a sales manager, part of your job description is psychologist and mediator. But you are first and foremost a nonjudgmental mentor and teacher.

Getting to the factual truth is one of the most important business skills to learn.

46

Pursue Excellence in these Four Areas: Spirituality, Academics, Physical Fitness, and Creativity

I know it sounds cliché, but I recommend having pursuits outside of your professional life in which you try to achieve excellence.

Those pursuits are in the areas of spirituality, academics, physical fitness, and creativity. I have to admit I'm a geek, and I just love to learn new things and how things work. Maintaining interests outside of work gives me a much needed respite from my professional life. It helps to keep me focused on what's most important (not work) and makes me a more well-rounded person.

Participating in non-work activities actually recharges my batteries and reignites my passion for work. I have a very short attention span, so I am constantly switching my areas of interest within each category.

How do I apply these in my own life?

Spirituality: Having been raised in a Christian household, I still continue that tradition and include prayers with my meditation practices every day. I find having a belief in God and a higher power truly gives me a great sense of self and perspective.

Academics: I'm always staying educated within my discipline, but here I'm talking about something outside my profession. I have a lifelong interest in languages, so I've been looking into learning Arabic and Spanish. Both of these can enhance my ability to service clients as well. I love history and biographies. I am constantly reading about men and women who have done great things and learning about their habits.

Physical fitness: I have run the gamut of exercise regimens over the years. I've done kickboxing, powerlifting, jiujitsu, hiking, and trail running. Every three or four months I lose interest in what I'm doing, so I find something else to do. I am still looking for the exercise guru who can make opening the refrigerator an aerobic activity.

Creativity: I guess it is apparent to everyone reading this that I truly enjoy writing and have since I was very young. I usually read historical nonfiction, though, instead of self-help or motivational books like this one. *Be The Chocolate Milk* is the second book I've published, the first being *Foxhole Father: The Field Guide For Fathers*. That is available on Amazon, and I urge everyone to buy a copy! Most often you will see my writing in short story form.

If you explore these enrichment areas—spirituality, academics, physical fitness, and creativity—you will be a much more interesting and well-rounded person. It will also allow you to expand your social and business circles, which is a great secondary benefit. I get clients from all of my personal pursuits. They are sometimes the best ones, as they share a personal passion with me.

So, are you pursuing something in all of these areas? If not, why don't you try to find something in all four areas?

Please write to me and let me know what you're doing in any or all of these areas at info@bethechocolatemilk.com.

47

Why Usually Doesn't Matter

You'll often hear me say that if someone is punching you in the face, it doesn't matter why, you just want it to stop.

That really explains what this chapter is all about, so it won't be a long one. So many people dwell on why things are happening. Sometimes that's important to know, but many times it is not.

So much time is wasted contemplating why. So many people are paralyzed from acting confidently in their best interest because they're pondering the motives and reasons behind things that have happened to them.

Try not to get emotional when things happen. Business is business. It is no time to inject your personal insecurities or worries into situations. That will only delay you in taking care of things and putting it behind you.

The most important thing is to take care of business right now and execute effectively and quickly. If you want to ponder the reasons why about things, sometimes it's better to do that at the end of the day while you're lying in bed.

If I am too emotionally involved in a situation, I will imagine my best friend is across the desk from me and asking advice as if this has happened to them. I then formulate the advice I would have given them and then I do that for myself. This is a great mental trick I have used for decades.

If something is wrong and you know it needs to stop, be mature and make it stop. Sometimes asking why someone has done or said something is just a psychological stall. Pausing is emotionally easier than executing. But you need to learn to be an executioner when it servers your best interest.

48

There Are Very Few People You Need to Answer To

In business and in life, if you answer to somebody, then they are your boss.

If you are working for a company right now, of course you need to answer to your direct supervisor or manager but very few others in the organization.

This is a topic very near and dear to me, because, believe it or not, at the heart of me, is someone who desperately wants to please people all of the time.

Now why do I make that seem like it's a negative? Because it is. It can lead you to care too much about what people think, and that may lead you to acting as if you need to answer to them or at least consider them in your decision making.

Just be conscious of this in your daily life and observe your interactions with other people. Are you answering to too many people? Do others seem to have authority over you when none is justified? Are you considering too many people in your decision making? Do others feel free to critique you?

Of course you need to service and assist clients, but especially with them exude the feeling that you are partnering with them and not answering to them. There is a difference, albeit a subtle one.

You may be surprised to discover that the more you objectively observe your interactions in your personal and business lives, the more you may not like what you see. Don't beat yourself up; just do the rare but mature thing and make the changes necessary to become the person you want the world to see.

Today, people are more imposing than ever and often feel free to comment on what someone else is doing. They may attempt to change someone's behavior by giving unwanted comments and advice.

This happened in my office parking lot recently. I parked my car, and an employee from a different company who was getting out of her car said, "I don't appreciate the way you park your car."

I didn't look towards her or acknowledge her in any way. I gave her no authority or respect in this situation, as she had none and deserved none.

Imagine all the time and money this saved me. I didn't allow her to monopolize my time by listening to her critique of my parking. The most important thing is that I didn't allow her to use me for her emotional satisfaction. Nor did I give her acknowledgement that she had authority over my parking. Again, because she has none.

49

Always Be Deliberate, Never Reactionary

This chapter is simply about impulse control. We all know people who explode at the slightest disappointment. There are some people I know who have the self-control of a four-year-old, constantly throwing tantrums and bringing negativity into other people's spaces. They are constantly oversharing.

I really want to urge you at all times to be self-observing. Imagine you are watching yourself from others' perspective. How would you react to someone who acts as you do? Would you respect that person?

This takes a lot of practice, but it is well worth it. It is very hard to be objective about yourself, but you need to be the greatest student of yourself in order to improve and become the most effective person you can be. Just taking a few moments to contemplate a situation, even a great emergency, can give you the greatest dividends and far better results than having knee-jerk reactions.

Do you have people around you that recoil to your negative reactions and your impulses? If so, instead of being defensive, try to take it as constructive criticism. You need to attract the best talent to work for you and the best clients to hire you. Reactionary people are not attractive, and the best clients, the best colleagues, and the best employees will avoid this type of person.

Ask people directly about how you handle yourself and about your overall demeanor. Ask if they see you as too reactionary and emotional.

As I have stated in the book, we can always use mentors. I use mentors to critique how I handle myself. I'll call a mentor and recount an interaction with someone. I'll be completely honest about how I handled myself, and ask them to give me their honest opinion.

I have found the more open I can be to constructive criticism and the more that I eliminate any defensiveness, the more I can continue to grow and learn as an entrepreneur.

You'll be surprised how much people appreciate it when you ask them for their personal opinions about something. It is a great compliment for someone to be asked this type of question, especially about their boss.

I role play upcoming conversations and meetings and do self-critiques. I create multiple answers and choose the best ones. I get ready for tough questions that may make me defensive, and I practice measured and calm responses.

If I misspoke during a conversation or a meeting, I will quickly call the other party to remedy that. I never want a negative interaction to linger in someone else's heart and mind against me.

So never be afraid to ask for constructive criticism. It is never a sign of weakness. It is a great sign of maturity and of respect for those around you, and they will truly appreciate it.

Becoming deliberate and not impulsive takes practice, but you can do it. The more you do this, the fewer things you will regret and need to apologize for.

50

When the Facts Change, I Change My Mind. What Do You Do, Sir?

Beware of fake (business) news and outdated internal systems.

Remember, today's absolute truth is tomorrow's debunked propaganda. What do I mean by this? The world is dynamic, and there is a fluidity with regard to facts.

Today, there is very little fact-checking and a lot of off-the-cuff sharing. Notice I don't call it reporting. Most of what I see, hear, and read from supposed news sources are unsubstantiated rumors and worthless opinions.

Just as Einstein disproved some of Isaac Newton's most important theories that were sacrosanct for centuries, we need to be skeptical, even about things we believe are etched in stone.

There are no foolproof systems or fully trustworthy information sources, as today there is no guarantee of journalistic integrity. There is no barrier any longer between reporting and the spread of propaganda. What looks like an independently written news story with sources vetted may be a well-crafted advertising piece.

Teach your staff to read everything with a healthy skepticism. Ask them to share articles that are truly helpful and pass editorial muster, but to avoid sharing those that are flimsy and border on fake news, advertising, or worse, propaganda. Entire web-based information companies (notice I didn't call them news outlets) are biased and push agendas. Be careful!

When I see a news article from a major news outlet that relates to what I do, with blatantly wrong information, I will prepare a memo citing it and correcting it. I may also send an email to important clients and customers with my analysis.

Internally, your codified systems should be under constant review. Every policy manual, systems manual, and work-related processing chart should be a living and evolving document. Urge your staff to be reading these with skepticism as well and to make suggestions for edits.

If you have an environment where people feel nurtured and supported and where their opinions are valued, they are more likely to provide you with input that will help streamline your organization's processes.

We have all had bosses closed off to suggestions regarding their rules. These bosses silence their staff who then become hesitant to share. Such a mistake! My staff is a constant source of feedback. I am not arrogant enough to think all of my answers are final or perfect. They are simply my best effort at the time.

51

It Takes a Village to Make an Entrepreneur

You are only as good as the team you surround yourself with.

Speakers, pundits, and coaches tell us we can be self-employed and eventually millionaires if we just decide to. But rarely will anyone tell you your talents and efforts are only a small part of the success equation.

So many things outside of you must fall into place in order for you to be a successful entrepreneur. So many people must put their energy into you.

Luck, connections, friendships, colleagues, teachers, family, and clients—all of these played as much a role as my own efforts, if not more sometimes, in building my business.

You are only one small component to your ultimate success as an entrepreneur or salesperson. Your success is dependent on many things besides your own efforts.

I suggest that you show great appreciation for everyone and everything around you and pay the mentoring you have received forward. Show and live your success humbly. Openly and consciously appreciate the hundreds if not thousands of others who have gotten you to where you are.

Every day I try to find ways to be a part of others' success.

I love bringing business owners together to do a deal, even when there is nothing in it for me. I consider my business world a village where we all are invested in a collective success. Mentoring others and facilitating deals for others is just as satisfying as closing my own deals.

52

Do Not Judge, Lest Ye Lose Business

In your business life, don't judge people, the markets, or society. You need to be an objective student and find ways to capitalize on that study. This is how you will learn to bring the greatest value to the world and profits into your enterprise.

In your personal life, let your biases have free reign, but at work, they need to be ignored.

I urge you to become a global student. What is happening in the world beyond your door? What are the trends in culture, fashion, politics, technology, sports, best business practices? All business is international to me. Our country is filled with immigrants. Learning about where they came from can only help you close deals. What are the business and social customs of the immigrants' homelands? Remember that children of first-generation immigrants are often taught the same traditions as their parents were taught and will respond with fondness to you if you are aware of them.

Also remember, the grandchild wants to remember what the parent wants to forget. In other words, a third-generation immigrant might be more influenced by their heritage than their parents are.

All of this "studying" can only help you sell "from the client," which, as you know, is one of the most important tenets of Be The Chocolate Milk.

No matter how local and small you feel your business radius is, gaining an understanding of global perspectives will enhance your ability to close business in so many ways.

Read periodicals and blogs and listen to podcasts of all types and of every political and cultural persuasion. Make sure you're reading foreign news sources. The news outlets in the U.S. do a very poor job of reporting news outside the country.

Many of us gravitate towards news and commentators that share our political views, and this is a mistake from a business perspective. You want to know how everyone on the planet is thinking and feeling. I especially listen to and read sources of news and analysis that are biased in ways that differ 180 degrees from my personal political or social biases. I personally lean towards libertarianism, but I love to listen to far left business and social commentary. I am constantly learning about ALL potential clients, and I am not looking for a political argument or for anyone in business to agree with my personal views. You should follow my lead here.

You may not think you have a global reach if you are not dealing with international customers, but your customers' hearts and minds may still dwell in their homeland.

America has the most diverse immigrant population in the world, which I believe, mostly, is a strength. Becoming a global student will help you understand more of the people you come in contact with, and that is the most important component to selling something to them.

Removing judgment from your business life and developing a global perspective should be daily goals.

53

You Are a Pencil

Whether you are an owner or an employee, you are someone else's pencil.

Employers don't have any true loyalty to you, nor do your clients. You are only a human "resource" to be used to further your company's or client's profit motive.

You're simply a pencil, an office supply. I want you to live in that emotional space and understand that every day. You pour your life and soul into your work, and when you perceive that you are underappreciated, it can be emotionally devastating. It is not your clients' job or your boss's job to appreciate you. They are supposed to use you and all your resources for THEIR greatest financial benefit and advancement. They are supposed to pay you what was agreed upon.

So, you need to be the best, most indispensable pencil! Or in other words, *Be The Chocolate Milk*.

This chapter is meant to protect you from the emotional upset you might feel when you see that you're not appreciated. Many will act like children and can be extremely needy of approval and praise. Remember your feelings of satisfaction or self-worth should never come from outside of you, whether that is from your clients, your boss, your mother, your significant other, etc. Avoid leaving your emotional system in the hands of things outside of you, especially people. That is always a disaster.

This chapter is about realizing your boss does not have to care about you or your best interest. The best managers don't care deeply or personally, as that will compromise their position. They can celebrate you one day and then fire you the next. This is not duplicitous or fake. Both gestures are sincere and meaningful.

To restate, your superiors and/or clients want to use you for your full potential and benefits for them.

Be emotionally prepared for that and remember: bosses who fire you and clients who leave you are not mean, and they haven't hurt you. You need to be mature. If you are feeling personally hurt, you need to self-observe and do all you can stop being the victim.

In business it should be business first, and that means you are also out to get all you can. Your bosses and clients are your pencils.

You have to make sure you're the answer to what people need more often than not. But you have to take away that feeling of deep personal allegiance and your need to have personal loyalty for your effort. Those types of feelings belong in personal relationships outside of work. In business you are always expendable; you are simply a pencil. But if you work hard, you will be the pencil they always reach for and cannot live without.

Again, your goal is to be the least expendable at all times. Budget cuts happen. Being The Chocolate Milk can make sure you are not one of them.

Unfortunately I have seen a sad trend in the past few years. Many college graduates are immature and incapable of functioning in a business environment. Many of them are extremely sensitive and cannot handle even the slightest suggestions, let alone criticism. The turnover rate of new college graduates is increasing.

Client Specific

54

Customer Complaints Can Create Customers for Life

Complaints can create future sales!

When faced with a complaint, your true professionalism can either shine or fade. The first decision you should make is: "Should I visit the client?" Emails and phone calls may not cut it, especially with your most profitable clients. Extending the offer to come to them can impress and shows your level of commitment to them.

This chapter suggests four things:

1) Never become defensive.
2) People don't need to praise you for doing your job; it is expected.
3) Strive to exceed expectations.
4) Use customer complaints to improve your business.

Don't expect to get accolades by doing your job correctly. You will rarely be praised for delivering what you promised.

You have to remember this when clients complain about your prodserv. It may seem counterintuitive, but these are the times when client retention truly happens.

Put yourself in their position. How would you want to be treated?

Customer complaints are a gold mine of information into the infrastructure and workings of your company on many levels. Take each of these as a chance to gain insight into your company and ways to improve it. Always approach a customer complaint with complete respect and understanding, by putting yourself in their place. Remember that these are emotional situations, and clients may not be thinking logically. An upset client may vent at you. Allow them to.

This is where understanding your client comes in handy. You'll hear my mantra that you need to be selling or servicing from the client at all times. If you've done that correctly, you will understand where this complaint is emanating from. You could get the same complaint from fifty different people, but always remember that each of these customers are different emotional beings. The emotions enveloping those complaints will always be different.

So as I've been trying to teach you, the ways of handling each complaint and the method used to pacify the client may be completely different each time.

First, how does the client believe our prodserv did not meet their expectations? Is their claim justified? Make it right. Is the claim unjustified? Then politely make them aware of that. But, most importantly, try to find out where the disconnect happened in those cases where you did deliver what was promised. For some reason this client's expectations do not coincide with the work that was agreed to. These moments are important teaching moments for your entire organization.

If your contract/engagement letter/invoice are clear enough, track down the employee who made the sale and, in a non-accusatory way, investigate what may have happened. Did a staff member miscommunicate?

Again, these moments are golden, and also free! Make the most of them.

Customer complaints are some of the best learning moments for you and your staff. Customer complaints need to be analyzed, and this information needs to be shared across your entire organization. This is actually free training information that can help your business be even more efficient and grow more quickly, so please take advantage of it.

My Basic Steps:

1. Listen patiently and sympathetically to the client without interruption.
2. Don't let your mind race ahead; stay focused on what they are saying.
3. Is the customer incorrect? Explain how. (Skip steps 4 through 8.)
4. Retrace steps in the process through the breakdown.
5. Identify causation.
6. Make it right with the client.
7. Alert your team to the glitch.
8. Implement a fix for the glitch.
9. Consider giving a partial or full refund, or fix for free.

It is very easy to get defensive, and no one would blame you. You feel you have done everything right: worked hard, done your very best, and cared about your client's best interest. And they are complaining now? How unappreciative!

Customer complaints are not about you.

Remember to take YOUR emotions out of it. Many people make the mistake of overestimating their client's devotion and connection with them. Most clients will leave you quickly for a better deal or attitude.

Your emotions and defensiveness can only further erode your client's satisfaction. Take time to self-observe during your interactions with colleagues and clients. Do you find yourself thinking and reacting emotionally instead of rationally? Are you more concerned about your best interest than your client's?

Do you overshare emotionally in business situations? Is this hurting your success?

Especially when a customer complains, you need to be a sympathetic listener who is the client's best advocate. Your feelings do not matter.

55

You Don't Want Every Client

Just like in personal relationships, not every client is a good fit. Work with clients who understand your value. See every new client meeting as an interview for a long-term relationship. Play out the next twenty years of having to deal with this person/company and see if it fits into YOUR business plan.

Many of you may say that a client with money to pay your invoice is a good fit. Yes, in some situations that may be true, but it really depends on the nature of your work. Even if your work entails selling generic prodservs, remember, all clients will take your time, and time is all you have to generate wealth for you and your family.

Just like in a romantic relationship, only invest your precious and LIMITED time and resources where they will lead to long-term profitable work now and in the future.

Part of your potential client interview process should include the questions:

1) Do I want to have a long-term relationship with this client?
    a) Will this client take more of my time or staff time than average per net profit dollar earned? Many professionals and salespeople don't incorporate this in their thinking about the profitability of clients, and that leads to costly mistakes in the future. If they will take above-average time and resources to service, it may be better to pass. Your time and staff's time will be better served elsewhere. Remember, these decisions will have an exponential financial impact over decades.
    b) Does this client's personality mesh with my corporate culture and staff sensibilities? We do need to keep clients happy, BUT if you force your staff to interact with distasteful clients, your staff may quickly move on to greener pastures. Many managers in the U.S. fail to consider the impact of clients on their staff. Don't make this mistake. Remember the circle of (business) life. The higher-quality clients you bring in will attract higher-quality staff who will attract higher-quality clients who will attract higher-quality staff. . . . You get the picture.
    c) How healthy is the potential client? How far in their business life cycle are they? Have you done some homework and research on this client and the principal owners and officers prior to meeting? No? Why not? Sometimes pre-meeting research has me cancel the meetings saving time and resources.

56

A Worried Client Is Not Judging You

It is so easy to get defensive and feel like a client is attacking us, when really they are just expressing their anxieties and fears. Be ready for these situations, as this is a time when your client needs you the most. More importantly it is the time that you can solidify your value in a client's life.

Envision your client base as a nursery of newborns, all crying at the top of their lungs. You would never feel judged when a baby is crying in a crib, correct? Apply the same emotional filter to a client who is worried and in need.

Your defensive or insecure reactions waste energy and time that should be spent pacifying the customer.

This baby-crying-in-a-crib analogy is to help you self-observe and control your emotional system so you can dispassionately formulate resolutions. Practice getting your feelings out of the way, and problems will get fixed much faster.

Observe yourself during the day in all your interactions. Make notes of how you are reacting. Do you find your personal feelings surfacing in situations where they should not be? Are you letting others see your personal feelings? This may be a mistake and may diminish others' respect for you.

As you have read or will read in this book, I practice such things every morning.

57

Let the Haters Hate (Somewhere Else)

You can never achieve 100% customer satisfaction, although it should always be your goal. After you have bent over backwards to make a situation right, don't spend more time trying to convince an entrenched negative customer of your value.

Identifying these types of people takes experience and wisdom.

It is easy to become insecure and defensive in these situations, and those emotional weaknesses may lead you to almost begging for this one customer's approval. This type of visible desperation can reduce your staff's respect of you.

Be extremely polite and accommodating, but your time may be much better spent providing a refund and taking back any prodserv and walking away.

Don't waste too much time allowing one person to occupy your emotional energy when the end result will not be any future business. Never try to win an argument unless it serves your goals.

No matter how we try to manage expectations, there are people who want to haggle and want to feel that they are in control. This will waste your time and energy if you are not careful.

Some people will never seem satisfied. They have a dysfunctional need to argue and find fault with things. This is a mental flaw within them and a form of emotional subjugation. Do you and your staff a favor, and politely fire them.

58

Charge Your Clients "Clients" as Well as Fees

When discussing billing with clients, I often discuss getting referrals from them. But how to do this without seeming to beg in desperation for more work?

I have approached this in many ways. Here is one example.

I explain that I spend much less time than others advertising and marketing. I go on to tell them this allows me to spend the majority of my time actually servicing my clients and giving the highest-quality services.

But, this approach, I explain, puts me at a disadvantage to my competition who spend more time marketing than actually focusing on their current clients' needs.

So, I let them know, tongue in cheek, that along with my monthly invoices, I am going to prepare another invoice, once per year, that simply reads: "Two Client Referrals."

This device puts a psychological obligation in a client's mind, and also sets up a true and tangible expectation with regard to referrals. This is very powerful and very effective. A satisfied client will gladly refer you.

Every month when billing and/or statements are sent out to clients, the number of "Referred clients still due" is included on a separate line item along with the monetary balance due.

I am not looking for lists of names here, and I am against ever doing that. I just would like my satisfied clients to ask colleagues, "Are you happy with your current CPA? If not, I would like to introduce you to mine."

59

Ask Your Clients for Testimonials and Reviews

When you see that a client is happy with your prodserv, that is a good time to ask them to prepare a testimonial or review for you.

These are great marketing tools for you that cost nothing.

At the same time, build a case study to be used for blog postings and staff training.

60

Partner with Everyone, Not Work for Them

I want to be seen as a partner with everyone. I foster this feeling even with my college interns. What does this mean? Well, partners are equal in many ways. Partners have an equal stake in the task at hand. Partners have a mutual respect based on equality.

My staff are not below me and my clients are not above me.

With clients you want to foster this idea, and earn the position of being their partner working with them, not for them.

Once you become The Chocolate Milk, you are elevated in your client's eyes.

If you don't become The Chocolate Milk and instead stay homogenized, then you will stay a vendor who is disposable and exchangeable and not a trusted and equal partner.

Strive to earn professional partnership with clients, and offer it to your staff.

61

Customers Should Be Compensated for Surveys and Feedback

Customer satisfaction surveys should not be executed immediately upon the delivery of a prodserv or at the end of a customer service phone call.

Surveys should inquire about the prodserv and not the support rep the customer dealt with. Businesses record all of the calls, so they can spend the money listening to calls later to evaluate their operators. It isn't my job.

How can I know how happy I am with a product five minutes after opening it? Those types of calls and emails should be delayed for a rational period of time.

After a customer service phone call for which my hold times were extreme, I should NEVER get an immediate call asking me how my experience was. That is insanely imposing and arrogant. My cellular carrier does this every time.

This is a terrible business practice, because no one is in their greatest mindset, even if their problem was resolved, immediately after ending a customer service or tech-support line call.

People want to get back to work, not answer a survey. If I was not satisfied with the support rep's work, I will simply call back to continue to attempt to get the problem resolved. Don't they realize that?

After you change your business practices here, maybe include an incentive. If a client or customer takes their valuable time to help YOU with your business, then they should be compensated. I don't know why companies don't understand this.

Your customers should not be expected to work for free.

When I am asked if I will take a brief survey after a customer service call, I always ask, "How much does that pay me?" and "Is there a discount off of my next purchase?" If both answers are no, I tell them I cannot afford to do that. I don't have that in my budget. My time is much too valuable.

We can turn the customer satisfaction survey into a productive and welcome thing, instead of the dreaded "avoid at all costs" monster it is now. Wouldn't you rather have one honest, detailed survey filled out by a customer who is financially and emotionally invested than a hundred completed out of duress?

As always, sell from the client. With regard to surveys, even the largest companies are not doing that.

Actions/ Processes

62

Delegate the Clerical

"You cannot sell unless you are selling." - Chris Whalen, CPA

That is my simple mantra during sales trainings and one of the most important lessons I can impart to any salesperson. And yes, even licensed professionals with their own practices—like doctors, lawyers, and CPAs—are salespeople first.

If a task doesn't directly increase sales, then delegate it. It is clerical. Salespeople should rarely be doing clerical tasks. Your strength is selling, and that is what you should be doing. Sales and marketing are the most important parts of an organization, and all other tasks are clerical ones that support them.

Quality control and new product development are a close second in importance to the sales department. This is something I usually workshop with my clients. I urge you to do the same over the next week.

Categorize the tasks you engage in into two columns.

Direct Selling Related	Clerical

You should continue to perform items in column 1 and delegate all you can in column 2. If your clerical column had many entries prior to this, you should see an increase in your sales volume.

Analyzing tasks and categorizing them will give you the ability to make the best use of your time and to maximize your sales.

If you are a salesperson, then you are not a clerical person. I want you to realize that, and I want you to make your bosses realize that. Worldwide, management puts too much clerical responsibility on salespeople. Then at month end, that salesperson receives complaints for a lack of performance! This is ridiculous and counterproductive.

If you have control issues and want to do everything yourself and not delegate anything, please seek professional mental help. You will never reach your full potential this way.

Do what you do best and delegate the rest.

Tell yourself and tell your boss what Chris Whalen, CPA has taught you: "I cannot sell unless I am selling."

63

Pre-Meeting Preparation

I want to be truly effective every moment. There is no fluff with me or wasted words or time, if I can help it. Whenever you can, try to gain some insight into your potential client prior to your sales meeting. Find out ahead of time how many of their staff will also be attending. What are their names? What are their positions? What is their level of authority? How long have they been in the company? What would be their relationship with you if you were engaged?

Request questions ahead of time from your point of contact and staff. Sending questionnaires can aid in this process and make people personally invested and excited.

Consider fact-finding phone calls before the meeting as well. These don't have to be too intense, but they offer you the chance to form a profile of the people you will be meeting with, and that is invaluable.

So much time is wasted in initial client meetings getting to know things about the client and their personnel before the actual selling can begin. This can easily be avoided by following the steps above.

Gather as much information on all of the players on the internet and through colleagues who may also know them. I have my assistant print out company website staff pages, and LinkedIn and Facebook pages. Remember, you want to be selling from the client (and client's staff), and you cannot do that if you know nothing about them.

What do these steps accomplish? Instead of having a canned presentation, we can have a customized presentation for all those who will be in attendance.

Too often, because we feel we're selling generic prodservs, we feel that our sales pitches can be generic. This is a very common mistake and needs to be avoided.

Isn't that a better idea? We can now start the meeting answering all of the questions and concerns provided to us.

Imagine how much more engaged all of the participants will be when they see you are prepared with answers to their direct needs and concerns. This is such an effective tool that I wish more people would use.

Doing some preparation ahead of time interacting with staff also increases the emotional anticipation of those personnel who will attend the meeting. It gets them emotionally invested in the process, and that is such a powerful selling tool.

Most of my sales meetings start with an effective presentation of real information and answers that the client and their staff need. Everything is customized, and I rarely come with a vague canned presentation.

64

Communicate Clearly, Not Hurriedly

As the speed and methods of communicating have increased the past thirty years, there has been a breakdown in the traditional formatting of correspondence. It would have been unheard of just a few decades ago to send a "communication" with no capital letters, as we do with texting daily.

Although this has made things easier, it also allows us to become sloppy and unclear. We can communicate instantly, and I believe that leads to unclear thoughts and messages being transmitted.

My point here is that you need to communicate clearly. Clear communication is one of my most important goals.

I have met many people who can speak the Queen's English, but who cannot clearly and concisely communicate what they are thinking.

With significant communications, I often ask the recipient to mirror back to me, in his or her own words, the message that person received from me.

I do this even during conversations, not just with emails and texts. This will tell me: 1) if the person is paying close attention, and 2) if they are clearly receiving my message.

I force myself to pretend that a traditionally typed letter is my fastest way of communicating. I act as if there is no instantaneous way to transmit my responses. I then craft and proofread my response, even with a text.

It is important to manage client expectations about how much time they should anticipate waiting for a response. If you respond too quickly, that sets up future expectations of the same response times. Also, if you respond within ten seconds to every client request, is it really possible you have adequately researched your answer?

An "I am working on it" text is a quick and easy way to let clients know you haven't forgotten about them.

65

Never Send Dynamic (Changeable) Files as Attachments

Quite often I see attachments in emails that are sent in DOC format or an XLS format. Unless you want the recipient to have the ability to change your information, I believe this is a big mistake, and I'll explain why.

Doc and XLS files are dynamic, meaning the recipient can change the content.

Every day, I receive resumes, business reports, and sensitive client financial information via email or online storage, and many of them are open to editing. It would be very easy for me to change some or all of the information in these cases.

An unscrupulous person could change a letterhead, detailed financial information, names, dates, etc., and then use a document for a nefarious purpose. It would seem that this information came from you when your original no longer exists.

Imagine how dangerous that is. Unless you are collaboratively working on a file with a colleague, I suggest you only send static documents such as PDFs as attachments. This does a number of positive things. Number one, a PDF is much more consistently viewable over platforms. Where you're going from PC-based to Apple products to desktops to tablets to mobile devices, a PDF is universally viewable and consistent, whereas viewing a DOC or XLS file is not always consistent. So the strength of your original message and your data could be unreadable or misinterpreted. Basically it could look like a mess.

There are many products that will quickly change your doc or XLS files to PDF for other static formats. Google Drive is my go-to app for conversions to pdf.

I highly recommend you do this before forwarding dynamic (changeable) files in the future.

66

Blind Copy Large Email Distribution Lists

We have all gotten emails that were sent to a large distribution list, and every other recipient is visible to us.

This happens when all recipients were listed as the main recipient of the email or they were CC'd.

It can look something like this:

Subject:	**Massive Distribution List Email**
To:	chriswhalencpa@gmail.com
CC:	xxxxx@email.com
	xxxxx@email.com
	xxxxx@email.com
	xxxxx@email.com
	xxxxx@email.com
	xxxxx@email.com
	xxxxx@email.com
	xxxxx@email.com
	xxxxx@email.com
	xxxxx@email.com
	xxxxx@email.com
	xxxxx@email.com
	xxxxx@email.com
	xxxxx@email.com
	xxxxx@email.com
	xxxxx@email.com

Email message starts way down here!

This is problematic for a few reasons.

1. It exposes every other email address to all other recipients, which many people don't appreciate, as it is a privacy breach.
2. It can sometimes force us to scroll down many pages to get to the actual email message content. As emails are often read on the smaller screens of tablets and phones, this can be a jumbled mess.
3. If other recipients "reply all," it can put us into that "group email death spiral" where every reply from every other recipient will hit our inbox.

The answer is simple.
When emailing a large group:

1. Use YOUR email address as the main TO: recipient.
2. BCC all other recipients. This hides their email addresses from all other recipients.

That way, all recipients only see your email and theirs. Everyone's privacy is protected, and the emails look much less cluttered with email addresses at the top. All the recipients will still see your email blast.

67

Schedule Distant Parking Locations Thirty Minutes before Appointment Times

Always consider your parking location and its distance from the meeting location when planning your travel time. Considering this will make you early for appointments more often.

Everyone knows my advice to be early. The further that you will need to park away from your ultimate destination for a meeting, the more extra time that you need to give yourself. I always like to arrive at least fifteen minutes early. That doesn't mean *park* fifteen minutes early, that means I am physically at the location and have announced my arrival to the receptionist.

Many parking locations are not directly adjacent to their related meeting locations. If there is a certain parking lot or garage, I make a separate calendar entry thirty minutes before the meeting time and make sure I include that specific address or GPS location. This eliminates having to search for the parking location.

It is disrespectful to be late for appointments. It shows a lack of professional discipline at worst and poor time management at best.

True time management is one of the most profitable skills you can learn. Good time management can eliminate the feeling of rushing all the time. Many people don't realize how rushed they are feeling all day, every day.

Make a habit of getting to your parking locations early. This will make you early for most appointments. It will ease scheduling-related anxiety, which many people suffer from.

68

Live Within Your Means

By now you know one of my mottos is "Desperation leads to self-compromise leads to enslavement." One of the easiest ways to become desperate is to not have cash reserves (savings). So in this chapter I want to make sure you are budgeting correctly and living within your means. That means the first line of your budgets is SAVINGS.

A good first savings goal is to have six months of both personal and business expenses saved in a bank account, not a brokerage account. This means cash immediately accessible. I don't care if you earn interest on it. You want to strive for this scenario: If you could not take in any income for six months, you could still live as you are now and run your business as you do now.

Planning like this will allow you to build the umbrella for that inevitable rainy day. That rainy day may be having a sudden personal expense or business capital expenditure you need to make. These "financial emergencies" are quite often the death knell for a business. If you don't have access to capital, either saved cash or a credit line (and many small businesses don't qualify for one), you may go under.

I have seen it happen many times.

You must live within your means personally and professionally. You must be ultra-conservative when it comes to your spending and plans for future spending.

This means asking questions like: "Do I take on extra staff right now? Do I get a better car that's more expensive? Do I buy a house or rent a house? Do I spend a lot of money on dating? Am I spending too much money socializing? Can I drive to my next vacation destination instead of flying to save the airfare?

Do you have a romantic partner or family member that is a financial drain? You may need to cut them loose.

Every dollar needs to be treated with the utmost respect. You worked hard to acquire it, so treat it that way. Surround yourself with others who also respect money and who are savers. Quite often our friends and family can believe that their financial deficits are also ours. Be sure to let them know that will never be the case.

Make sure you are putting SAVINGS on the very first line of both your personal and business budgets. Make this a mandatory item along with the other minimum budgeted items such as rent, insurance, and utilities.

When it starts to rain, and your planned-for financial umbrella opens above you, you will think back to this chapter fondly and with appreciation.

Remember, six months of cash in the bank for both personal and business expenses is your savings goal.

69

Be Early

1. Be early for meetings.
    a. Why?
        i. Pick the seat with the best vantage point and sight lines with power players.
        ii. Have pre-meeting conversations with meeting hosts and other early arrivers to glean inside information others do not know.
        iii. Others who come after you will see you have arrived and are settled in, putting you in a perceived power position.

2. Be early with deliverables.
    a. Why?
        i. Beating project delivery time expectations never fails to impress.
        ii. Or, get deliverables done ahead of time, still deliver at expected project delivery time, then use the extra time

cushion to meditate, sleep, go to a movie, or work out.

3. Be early for the train.
    a. Why?
        i. Get the best seat nearest the exit to expedite your exit upon arrival at your destination.

4. Be early with birthday and anniversary greetings for your partner and staff.
    a. Why?
        i. A birthday remembered is appreciated. A birthday remembered ahead of time evokes love and surprise and loyalty.

5. Be early for your workout.
    a. Why?
        i. Assume that important machines will be occupied, causing your wait times to be extended. If you are not early, your workout could be cut short.

6. Be early to bed.
    a. Why?
        i. Deep, restful, and recuperative sleep is the most important business tool we have.

7. Be early.
    a. Why?
        i. Being late always looks bad.

70

Reserve the Right to Answer Your Phone at All Times

Reserve the right to answer your phone at all times. It could be money calling you, and that is more important than most meetings you are participating in.

Now, in client meetings use your best judgement, but try to answer business calls during staff meetings, seminars, or trainings. Remember, you're looking to get new business, service existing clients, and also to put fires out. You can't do those when you don't answer your phone.

Technically a staff meeting's goal is to make your phone ring. So, isn't your phone ringing during that meeting a sign these meetings work? Our phone ringing is the critical moment we are all waiting for!

Do you understand what I'm saying? Any client interaction has to become the priority. Even if I'm sitting with another client, I usually pick up my phone. New clients who have an old school mentality initially get annoyed and feel disrespected when I do this. But when I explain to them that when they called me the day before and I picked up the phone that I was sitting with another client, they quickly begin to understand how this helps the entire community of my clients continue to work.

Now I don't take a very long phone call in those cases, but if I can possibly take care of another client's need within a minute or two, or I can let them know I will get right back to them, it does not greatly infringe on the time of the client sitting with me.

Handling calls this way has an overwhelmingly positive impact on my clients. In a world where it is so difficult to get someone to call you back, it seems to my clients that I am just waiting for their call and seemingly in the cubicle next to them.

Voicemails are a tremendous waste of time. Remember, many times my clients can't continue working without my input. That is why they are calling. So the client who is immediately at need is technically more significant and deserves my immediate attention more than someone I am having a meeting with.

Imagine I didn't take the phone call but did what is traditionally done and allowed my voice mailbox to fill up. What am I left with then after my meetings? First, I'm left with clients who are stalled in their efforts to build their business. Secondly, I am now left with a block of time where I need to attempt to call those people back. What happens if I cannot get them on the phone? That means I leave them a voicemail!

So answering that initial phone call, even during a meeting, is the best time to answer. It is also the most efficient use of my time and increases client satisfaction.

Now my newer clients, when we have future meetings and my phone rings, tell me to pick up the phone! They quickly begin to realize my wisdom and how this makes everyone more efficient.

Back to staff meetings. I want my staff to take any business call that comes in, especially during meetings. This gives me a window into the client relationship that I wouldn't normally see, and it gives other staff some real-time training. Both of these things are so helpful.

I am asked to speak often. I specifically bring this up at the start every time. I tell the audience I have cell phone rules when I speak. I see everyone start to reach to silence their phones. I continue and tell them they must make sure they can hear their phone and answer it during my presentation, as any call they may get is much more important than what I am saying.

I then say I will be doing the same, as that person calling me is probably a paying client, and the audience members aren't yet. Laughter ensues. Most importantly I haven't treated adults like children who need to be told how to behave.

I close this chapter as I opened it: Make sure you answer your phone, even in meetings. It could be money calling you, and that is more important than most meetings you are participating in.

71

Never Celebrate Early or in Front of the Competition

This would seem to be common sense. But I learned it the hard way and at great cost early in my career. The first part, never celebrating early, is so important. Always be 100% sure that:

1. The deal went through.
2. The client accepted the engagement with a signed engagement letter.
3. The check has cleared as opposed to just having been received!

That last one is very important. Some checks are not worth the paper they're printed on.

Celebrating early may make you put things in motion that shouldn't be in motion yet. It may make you expend money you really haven't earned.

And never gloat to the competition that you've just beaten. Humility is always the best approach to most situations. There are some people who love for the competition to know the accounts they have won.

You should just let your good standing and good reputation speak for itself in the marketplace. Try not to discuss your conquests in business social circles, at least not in such a way that it appears you're boasting.

Lastly, today's competition could be tomorrow's business partner. Treating adversaries with respect can only see that respect mirrored back at you.

In my practice I support attorneys in many types of cases. They are mostly adversarial, and the contempt I can feel from the opposing counsel and accountants is palpable. But, once the case is done, many of those same attorneys I was passionately fighting with will call to engage my firm.

Even in those high-stress situations, where so much is on the line, I know that I am still selling every moment to everyone I come in contact with.

Everyone on the planet is either my client, or about to become one.

72

Mentors Are Vital: Get One Today, Be One Today

You are mentoring everyone subordinate to you. Most business owners/managers don't see it that way, but they should.

Just using the word "mentor" elevates the level of your responsibility greatly. Try to make your staff better versions of themselves along with getting the most productivity from them. You want them to look back years from now and see you as the gold standard of teachers they have had, not just a former boss. Make sure they take as much of your accumulated experience with them when you part company.

Always demand excellence and hard work, but do it with the greatest kindness, respect, and sincere appreciation.

An ounce of training is worth a pound of profit for both of you.

How do your staff view you? If they were to write a reference for you, and not vice versa, what would it say?

Make sure your staff understands WHY they are completing a task and not just the steps to get something done. They should understand how their tasks fit into the bigger picture of your processes and ultimate prodserv.

If an employee seems to be having trouble completing a task based on your directions, many times you are to blame. Yes, it is possible they cannot grasp the subject matter, and then you are still to blame as that is an error in hiring.

People beneath you deserve patience and understanding. Just as we should be selling from the client, we need to be training from the employee. Not everyone learns the same way. Some people love a hands-on instructor, while others prefer reading an instruction manual and completing review tests. Others like online automated courses.

Take the time to understand the emotional and psychological sensibilities of your subordinates.

Be flexible in your approach to everything, especially training.

No matter how successful you feel you are, you can still benefit greatly from finding mentors. Seek them out for yourself! I have mentors in both business and my personal life.

Always be open to learning. Realize that what you consider successful business and personal practices can be made even more effective when looked at through the seasoned and wise eye of a mentor.

73

On Presenting with Other Speakers

Simple rules:

1. Be selective. Those you present with are a reflection on you. When necessary, be strong enough to decline invitations to co-present.
2. Does it make sense that you are presenting together? Do the topics mesh?
3. Review other presenters' content. Most times I present on my own. But, when I am collaborating with others, I make sure we compare notes and customize content to have a more seamless and blended overall message. I try my best to mention the other speakers in the body of my segment.
4. Have a full run-through so there are no surprises for you and final tweaks can be made.
5. Order the speakers from weakest to strongest (least effective to most effective).
6. Be the closer.
7. Leave the audience wanting more.

74

If You Are a Reactor, You Are Already Behind and Most Likely Lost

Reactors all eventually melt down. The marketplace and your competition should be reacting to you and not vice versa.

I say this many different ways:

- Be a deliberate actor, not a mindless reactor.
- Leaders act, followers react.
- Reactors are eating other people's dust.

You need to be a student of your industry and to start anticipating things. What is the next trend? How can I capitalize on it? Why don't I make the next trend?

If you become a student of the marketplace and not simply a prodserv provider, then your intuition will naturally grow. You will begin to see there are things clients need that you weren't aware of.

This is where the best sales come from and how you transform from a homogenous gallon of milk to The Chocolate Milk.

Do you find yourself surprised by what the competition is doing? Then you are probably a reactor playing catch-up.

75

Need to Vent? Do it Safely and Privately

Most times when we are upset and choose to vent at someone in our work environments we regret it. How do I handle frustrations with people? In the moment I know I need to vent, this is what I do. I open a scratch document and start typing furiously! I let the person have it in the privacy of my own space.

But a warning! If you are enraged from an email you just received, do NOT hit the reply button and vent with no intentions of hitting send! You can easily send it by accident. So close your email program completely, and open up a blank document on your local computer. Sometimes I just used WordPad. Then I write a response that only I can see. I usually save those and revisit them a week later to see if I still want to send them. Almost 100% of the time I delete them, and I am extremely glad I exercised restraint.

Another suggestion is to open a voice recording app on your phone and, with the windows closed, vent as loudly and for as long as you need to. Some may ask "Why do I need to use the recorder?" I know I would feel odd talking to myself in the car. Using the phone this way is completely natural and it makes us feel as if we are having a discussion with someone. Which is exactly how we want to feel—as if we are yelling at someone without them interrupting us!

You can save that audio recording like the typed document above and revisit it at a later date to see if you still want to have that conversation.

At these moments we simply need to express ourselves and enjoy the emotional and psychological release that gives us. We now have gotten that release, but without the fallout of attacking someone.

And remember, mentors are the best sounding board and love to hear your frustrations. Consider calling them in these situations.

I urge you to also self-observe in these situations. No one should be able to get you to the point where you want to scream, at work or at home. Try to avoid this emotional escalation in yourself as it is very unhealthy. One of my daily goals is to not let anything outside of me impact my emotions in a negative way.

Technology

76

Make the Most of Your Calendar

All too often people have separate systems to keep track of things when they could simply be using their calendar for all of them. Using one piece of software can more fully automate your processes and stop you from having to jump from program to program to get things done.

There is some great time and project management software available. However, I find many of those have functionality that most of us will never have a need for.

We have calendars, planners, project software, reminders, time and billing or work-in-process systems and to-do lists. Do yourself a favor and use your calendar for as many of these tasks as possible. If your calendar's functionality, including the hacks I describe here, eventually do not serve you effectively, then it is time to look for a new software (but not before, in my estimation).

For example, I use my calendar for follow-ups where I set the time frame as all day and use FU and a description.

For example: FU - Jill Johnson Rental Property Questions. Setting an all-day timeframe means that those calendar events are going to come up first for that day, giving me a to-do list or fires to put out, and my scheduled appointments come after. This is perfect for most of us. I keep notes within those FU entries, and if I need to, I can move this quickly to a day in the future to follow up again. Just before I execute an FU, I will open up the entry and see my accumulated notes so I am ready to be effective on the FU call or email.

I can use a similar all-day event for staff related work. For example, an FU for my employee Anthony Lynch might look like this: FU AL - Smith Project Update.

In my business I need to keep track of my staff's billable time, or my work in process. I bill every two weeks. So I set up an invoice calendar entry with an all-day time frame and will use that to accumulate work-in-process time and billing information. I then use that to build my invoices semi-monthly.

I have an assistant review all timesheets daily and then update or create invoice calendar entries. When mid-month or end-of-month comes, I am ready to use that information to create invoices.

Another little trick I invented is a daily all-day event that has the words "DONE DONE DONE DONE DONE" in the description. This I color in red. Once a day is truly done, meaning I have completed all tasks shown or moved them to a future date, I simply change the ending day of this event to that day.

So what does this do? Let me show you a screenshot. Now when I am looking at an entire month I can quickly know what days I don't need to look at as they are "DONE." This can save a tremendous amount of time.

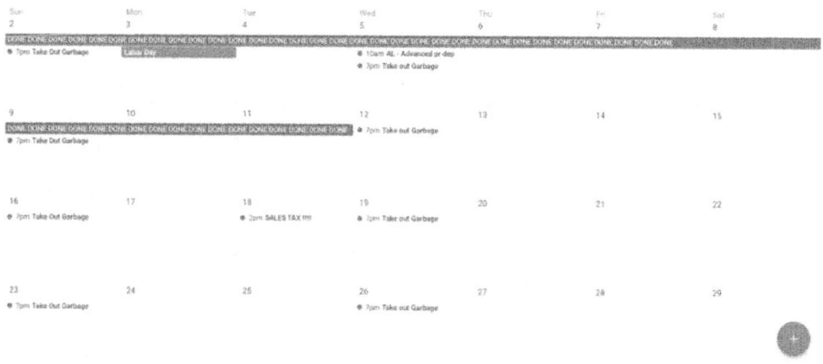

I'm always looking to save as much time as possible. Let's say you're looking at your calendar in "month" view. Having this DONE header and having it colored brightly, such as in red, will allow your eye to ignore those dates and simply look at active dates with open calendar items.

I also can see all of my staff's calendars, either individually or overlaid with others. This allows me to suggest changes when necessary. My firm is a dynamic organism existing in an international ecosystem. Nothing is static. You must be ready to answer to this marketplace ecosystem instantaneously. That often means moving your human resources.

These are just a few things that you should be doing with your calendar. If you use the Google system, the Google Calendar will allow you to also show reminders.

The takeaway from this is that you want all of your to-do items, reminders, fires to put out, FUs (follow ups), work in process, and actual scheduled events to come up in one app and in one place with no need to look elsewhere.

If you need to look in different places, it is very easy to miss something, and it is always a time waster.

77

Voicemail

If you have a voicemail system that gets full and stops being able to take messages, replace it immediately. A full voicemail box screams so many negative things about you I cannot list them all, but here are a few:

People may think you are:

1. Lazy
2. Inept
3. Not interested in their needs
4. Not working full time in your position

Not allowing a client to leave you a message is a mistake. It basically says, "Shut up! Don't call me! Your needs are insignificant!"

Think about when this has happened to you, and how much of your time was wasted. You had to listen to twenty or more seconds of rings, then the voicemail announcement message, only to be shut down. Sometimes this process takes more than a minute. Don't ever waste your client's time like this.

Get Visual Voicemail with unlimited storage. Visual voicemail is a voicemail inbox that not only shows you the caller, but also transcribes the messages and gives you an inbox similar to an email system. It also allows you to listen to your message in any order.

The days of dialing into voicemail and listening to messages are long gone. You want to see all of your missed calls, with transcriptions, in a neat list and triage them. Still using a voicemail system where you need to "dial in" to get your messages? What if the tenth call is the most important one? Wouldn't you want to quickly see that one, instead of going through the nine message before?

Visual voicemail will let you scroll through all messages and read them quickly.

Do you have to call everyone back? Many times you don't. If a quicker and less intrusive communication method is available, use that. I have a texting app open in my browser as I work at my desk. Many voicemails can be answered with a direct text. I do this often. Next step would be an email. Make sure you have every possible communication tool at the ready, whether at your desk or on the go.

Remember, every communication is a new first impression. This is often lost on salespeople and professionals, especially with their older clients. I treat every client interaction as if it is the first, and I want to ensure that I impress, educate, and reflect that I am the man for the job at hand.

Visual voicemail is an excellent tool. Used the right way, it will decrease response time and enhance your clients' experience with you. This leads to increased client retention and the generation of new business through referrals from them.

My preferred visual voicemail is Google Voice.

Is your voice mailbox full right now? Do you even know? Come on, be honest. If so, follow the easy steps of this chapter.

78

Gmail Is an Email Client Like Outlook: Use It

Many people don't realize Gmail can be used just like Outlook, as an email client. The Gmail client has fantastic spam filters and time-saving functionality.

This includes filters, labels, canned responses, etc., to name only a few features.

1. Smart Reply
    - This feature suggests three quick responses to emails you receive. Smart Reply utilizes machine learning to give you better responses the more you use it. This feature appears automatically to all Gmail users, but it can be turned off.

2. Mute a Group Email
    - Have an email thread no longer relevant to you? Mute it so future responses do not enter your inbox.

3. Labs in Gmail
    - Labs enable you to customize your mail experience. Take the time to learn all about them. They can truly enhance your productivity and reduce the time spent reading and answering emails.

4. Undo Send
    - You can recall an email you sent. Gmail will delay the email being sent by five, ten, twenty, or thirty seconds, giving you time to "undo" sending the email within the grace period you set up. This feature is in your Settings (the gear icon) on the General page.

5. Add a Meeting Directly to Calendar from Email
    - Event dates and times can be clicked on within an email to open your calendar and create an event. This is a great time saver.

6. Labels
    - You can organize your emails by setting up labels. Labels work like folders, but you can add more than one label to a message. Labels are a great way to see all emails related to one project/client/matter. For example, you can automatically have emails from certain email addresses or emails containing a keyword assigned a specific label based on that address or keyword.

For example, I have labels for:

- Faxes: incoming and outgoing faxes
- Resumes: resumes I am reviewing
- BTCM: emails related to publishing this book.
- xmas: emails with invoice receipts for Christmas presents for my daughters

When I have extended projects with many players, I set up a temporary label, which I will eventually delete. For example, let's say I was just hired to perform a forensic investigation in an embezzlement case for a client named LaForgia. I will create a label called LaForgia Embezzler, and all emails that relate to that topic can easily be labeled that way. This will give me the entire email history of this matter whenever I need it. Once the case is done, I delete the label, but of course the emails are retained.

Learn all the functionality of your apps and devices. Read all instruction manuals cover to cover at least once, making notes of functionality that can streamline your work.

You can get all of the power of Gmail and still use your existing email address. So, if you are unhappy with your current email experience, check it out.

79

Learn All Features of Any New Device or App

Whenever I get a new device such as a computer, Chromebook, phone, or tablet, I always read through the entire instruction manual.

You would be surprised how many new functions people are not aware of and how much time they are NOT saving due to this. Every new generation of a device will have greater functionality.

I track my time in keystrokes and swipes. Learning all functionality of your devices and apps can save you thousands of these each week.

How many of you don't even open the instruction manuals? Come on, be honest.

Another thing you can do is search online for the top ten tips and tricks for your device. Those types of websites pop up very quickly after a new device is announced. You will find countless videos explaining the new benefits and functionality, as well as any bugs that may be lurking.

It will definitely be time well spent, enabling you to get the most effective use of your devices from now on.

What good is a new device if it doesn't save us time and help us do our jobs more effectively?

My devices and apps are my most important business tools.

80

Keyboard Shortcuts Can Save You an Incredible Amount of Time

IMPORTANT NOTE: Like any other habit, it takes several weeks of deliberate use of keyboard shortcuts to make them second nature. I want you to trust me that using these will lead to time savings and better accuracy. Take your time, experiment, and use these in as many situations as you can. Especially with typing, there are so many ways to speed up your work by using shortcuts.

These are just some basics to get you started.

For Windows:

Shortcut	Keys Description
Alt+F	File menu options in current program
Alt+E	Edit options in current program
Alt+Tab	Switch between open programs
F1	Universal Help in almost every Windows program
F2	Rename a selected file
F5	Refresh the current program window

Ctrl+N	Create a new, blank document in some software programs
Ctrl+O	Open a file in current software program
Ctrl+A	Select all text
Ctrl+B	Change selected text to Bold
Ctrl+I	Change selected text to Italics
Ctrl+U	Change selected text to Underlined
Ctrl+F	Open "Find" window for current document or window
Ctrl+S	Save current document file
Ctrl+X	Cut selected item
Shift+Del	Cut selected item
Ctrl+C	Copy selected item
Ctrl+Ins	Copy selected item
Ctrl+V	Paste
Shift+Ins	Paste
Ctrl+Y	Redo last action
Ctrl+Z	Undo last action
Ctrl+K	Insert hyperlink for selected text
Ctrl+P	Print the current page or document
Home	Goes to beginning of current line
Ctrl+Home	Goes to beginning of document
End	Goes to end of current line
Ctrl+End	Goes to end of document
Shift+Home	Highlights from current position to beginning of line
Shift+End	Highlights from current position to end of line
Ctrl+Left arrow	Moves one word to the left at a time
Ctrl+Right arrow	Moves one word to the right at a time
Ctrl+Esc	Opens the START menu
Ctrl+Shift+Esc	Opens Windows Task Manager
Alt+F4	Close the currently active program
Alt+Enter	Open Properties for the selected item (file, folder, shortcut, etc.)

For Mac:
Keyboard Shortcuts

By pressing a combination of keys, you can do things that normally need a mouse, trackpad, or other input device.

To use a keyboard shortcut, hold down one or more modifier keys while pressing the last key of the shortcut. For example, to use the shortcut Command-C (copy), hold down Command, press C, then release both keys. Mac menus and keyboards often use symbols for certain keys, including the modifier keys:

Command ⌘	Shift ⇧	Option ⌥
Control ^	Caps Lock ⇪	Fn

Cut, copy, paste, and other common Mac shortcuts:

Shortcut	Description
Command-X	Cut the selected item and copy it to the Clipboard.
Command-C	Copy the selected item to the Clipboard. This also works for files in the Finder.
Command-V	Paste the contents of the Clipboard into the current document or app. This also works for files in the Finder.
Command-Z	Undo the previous command. You can then press Command-Shift-Z to redo, reversing the undo command. In some apps, you can undo and redo multiple commands.
Command-A	Select all items.
Command-F	Find items in a document or open a Find window.
Command-G	Find Again: Find the next occurrence of the item previously found. To find the previous occurrence, press Command-Shift-G.

Command-H	Hide the windows of the front app. To view the front app but hide all other apps, press Command-Option-H.
Command-M	Minimize the front window to the Dock. To minimize all windows of the front app, press Command-Option-M.
Command-N	New: Open a new document or window.
Command-O	Open the selected item, or open a dialog to select a file to open.
Command-P	Print the current document.
Command-S	Save the current document.
Command-W	Close the front window. To close all windows of the app, press Command-Option-W.
Command-Q	Quit the app.
Option-Command-Esc	Force Quit: Choose an app to force quit. Or press Command-Shift-Option-Esc and hold for three seconds to force just the front app to quit.
Command–Space bar	Spotlight: Show or hide the Spotlight search field. To perform a Spotlight search from a Finder window, press Command–Option–Space bar. If you use multiple input sources to type in different languages, these shortcuts change input sources instead of showing Spotlight.
Space bar	Quick Look: Use Quick Look to preview the selected item.
Command-Tab	Switch apps: Switch to the next most recently used app among your open apps.
Shift-Command-Tilde (~)	Switch windows: Switch to the next most recently used window of the front app.
Shift-Command-3	Screenshot: Take a screenshot of the entire screen. Learn more screenshot shortcuts.
Command-Comma (,)	Preferences: Open preferences for the front app.

81

Use Voice Recognition as Much as Possible

I use voice recognition for dictation, text messaging, emails, and web lookups.

In the car it is especially important to stay hands-free for safety. There are many applications for your phone that use voice commands and even hand gestures so that you do not need to physically use your hands to communicate while driving.

It is unrealistic to think people will not text or email while they're driving. So please download apps to keep you safe and hands-free.

The words you are reading right now were dictated into my Chromebook using voice recognition.

Don't have a microphone on your computer? Don't have voice recognition or dictation software loaded? Well if you use Google Drive and load the app on your phone, you don't need them.

Quite often I will open a document on my phone in Google Drive when I'm behind the wheel and turn on voice recognition. I can then dictate correspondence, memos, project notes, or chapters of a book without taking my eyes off the road.

Also, I can be at my desk and have that document open on my desktop's screen. I then open the same document on my phone and use that microphone to dictate and watch as the words appear on my desktop screen. So you don't even need to have a microphone on your computer. Your phone acts as one.

82

Use Free Conference Call Systems

When you're planning to make a phone call with more than one person, I strongly urge you to establish an account with one of the many free conference call systems. You can then provide all of the participants with the phone number and login information.

This will enhance the quality of your conference calls. All too often participants in conference calls are merging calls on their cell phones or their office systems. This can lead to different levels of voice volumes as well as hit or miss connection quality.

So whenever you have more than one participant on the call, make sure to use a conference call system. A nice feature of these systems is they email you a report afterward that tells you how long the conference call lasted and the phone numbers of the participants.

This is vital information you should retain. If you are billing by the hour, it is perfect support for that billable time you just spent on behalf of a client.

When you participate in a conference call with more than a few callers, many of whom will be mostly just listening, ask those parties to mute their phones. This will stop stray noises coming through their phones. I have been on conference calls in this situation when the phones are not muted, and the accumulated background noise of so many phones can drown out the people who are speaking.

83

Use Dialing Shortcuts to Automate Calling and Save Time

Are there people you call regularly for whom you need to enter an extension?

Do you call into conference call systems and need to remember the unique code to enter the conference?

There are ways to automate this process, which will save you a lot of time.

Let me introduce you to two special characters you can insert into your contacts' phone numbers.

, Comma - This inserts a two-second pause.

; Semi-Colon - This inserts a wait or pause, meaning you will be prompted when to continue.

Here is how these work in real life.

I call my client Joe D at work often, and he is at extension 41. His company has an automated attendant, which we all have heard a million times: "Please enter your party's extension." Traditionally I would then press 41 and be connected. But, if we know we have to do that every time we call Joe, why don't we automate it?

In my contact entry for Joe, his phone number looks like this:

732-555-4165,,41

This calls his company's main number, pauses four seconds, and then enters 41 automatically. My call is connected. I only have to call his number; the rest is automated.

I have a conference call system that I use almost daily. I have to enter additional information on top of the general login, as I am the moderator (owner) of the call.

I have automated this entire process as follows:

1-800-555-3237;167732598#;*;3247#

What does this do?

Dials 1-800-555-3237

;	Pauses and waits for me to push a button to continue sending my dialing sequence
167732598#	Sends 167732598#, my unique conference call code followed by the # sign.
;	Pauses and waits for me to push a button to continue sending my dialing sequence
*;	Send * and waits for me to push a button to continue sending my dialing sequence
3247#	Sends 3247#, my unique conference call PIN, followed by the # sign.

This connects me into the conference call.

This is very helpful with customer service support lines where you need to enter your customer code each time you call.

Try to find other ways to use these shortcuts to save time.

84

Time Zones: Set Your Devices to the Correct One

Have you ever found that the times of calendar events that were shared with you did not seem to coincide with what you agreed to?

Many calendar programs will convert the time of an appointment that has been shared with you to the time zone on your device.

This is fantastic if you're in a different time zone than the person you have scheduled a calendar event with. But I'm finding that many devices are not set to automatically find the correct time zone, so the time you're being shown on your calendar for an appointment you've accepted is actually not correct.

Some devices are set to GMT or UCT, for example.

So take the time right now to make sure the time zone settings are correct on all of your devices, including your computers, tablets, and smartphones.

Some devices have a setting to automatically pick your time zone based on GPS locations. I urge you to purposefully select your exact time zone as the automatic functionality is not always reliable.

85

Subscribe to Tech Blogs

Technology is changing every day. In order to stay ahead of my competition, I subscribe to some informative technology-related blogs. These include video blogs as well as traditional blogs.

Technology is one discipline we all use, regardless of our professions.

I subscribe to technology-related blogs such as:

- Industry specific tech blogs (accounting, business, etc.)
- New device announcements and reviews
- New app announcements and reviews
- Blogs for the specific hardware and software I use daily
- Top tech under $50.00

Set up news alerts for your devices and most used programs. For example, I have Google News alert for all of mine. I then get an email when the important tools I use are in the news or mentioned in a blog.

It is worthwhile to get alerted to tips and tricks, updates, recalls, etc. This will help you get the most out of your devices.

86

Check Business Social Media Accounts on a Schedule

Many of us feel we are missing something if we aren't constantly checking our social media accounts. This mistake can waste a lot of valuable work time.

I don't have alerts on my phone or my computer for social media notifications, but I do have alerts if someone has messaged me, of course.

I will check my social media accounts at the end of the morning and a half hour before leaving the office. That means Facebook, LinkedIn and Instagram feeds, among others.

When I have clients keep track of their internet usage, they are always surprised how much time they are NOT spending productively. I urge you to temporarily run a program that keeps track of your internet usage all day. It can be eye-opening.

This chapter title should have been "Check Business Social Media Accounts on a Schedule and Personal Ones After Work Only." But it would have taken up too much space.

87

Digital Disaster Recovery/Redundant Systems Save Businesses

Imagine you pulled up to your office tomorrow and found a burnt-out shell—A TOTAL LOSS.

Your computers, systems, and all paper files are gone. On-site backup is gone.

Where would you do business? How long would it take you to restore your systems and data from backups and be ready to service your client base?

If you are not sure, or your answer is more than just a few hours, I urge you to put backup protocols in place and to test them, so your time down due to a hardware, software, and paper file loss will be unnoticeable to your clients.

I have seen business disruptions less severe than what I described above put companies out of business. Clients have no allegiance, and the moment they feel you are professionally compromised, they will walk.

In what situations do you need redundant systems?

1. Office burns down:
    a. How long will it take you to service your clients if your entire office and its contents no longer exist? If more than four hours, then you need to put a Disaster Recovery Plan in place and not just a Digital Disaster Recovery plan.

2. Cell phone stops working, and data on it is not accessible:
    a. Always keep your last cell phone you upgraded from. Simply move the SIM card to the old one and power it up. If you don't have your old one because it was broken or lost, purchase a cheap backup online.

3. Key person leaves/quits/dies:
    a. All too often companies leave too much of their future success in the hands and minds of one or a few individuals. This leads to:
        i. A complete imbalance of power
        ii. A future that is no longer in your hands
        iii. A disaster when one of those people quits
            1. Battle this with redundant training of employees and ongoing evaluation of that training.
            2. Also ensure that procedures and systems are codified so there is a roadmap for a key person's replacement.

4. Do you only use one supplier for your products?
    a. What if that supplier has not read this book and has a disaster? How long would it take you to replace your product stream? If you say longer than one day, you have a problem.
        i. Contact your main suppliers and ask them what systems they have implemented to assure a constant stream of products to you in case of disaster. Make sure they send you the details of the actual tests conducted. Don't just take their word for it.
    b. Make sure to maintain at least two suppliers concurrently for your main products. Never just rely on one. Many companies fall into the trap of using one main supplier, usually due to price. The lowest price gets all the orders. But, depending on your business, paying slightly extra for some of your product could be a great investment, especially when disaster strikes.
        i. For example, I have three accounting placement agencies on rotation so my staffing needs, especially during tax season, can be filled.

To restate, TEST, TEST, and RETEST your disaster recovery systems once they are in place. Perform drills every quarter. Just putting disaster recovery systems in place is not enough.

88

Signatures on Email and Texts Should Be as Short as Possible

The signatures I am talking about are the automated ones you include on emails and texts.

The first thing to do with your signatures is to take Strunk & White's advice and eliminate unnecessary words (and images). I see many email signatures with quotes, pictures, and logos. If you have a logo that is small enough, keep that.

These take up a lot of space, especially the pictures and logos. Many people read their emails on phones and tablets. When you have an email thread that starts to get many responses back and forth, your signature will be repeated each time. These can start to take up an inordinate amount of room and make the threads unreadable at times. You want to avoid that.

Take an objective look now. Are your signatures taking up unnecessary room? They may be a heavy burden to the reader.

Again, this comes down to respecting people and their time. My email signature is three lines with no pictures.

My Name

Phone Number

Website

Your email signature should never be longer than your average email.

I don't have a text message signature at all. Even the smallest text signature can make text threads onerous and unreadable. When I see them, I request the other party remove them. If they won't, I move the conversation to email.

Quotes can make you look pompous, immature, unprofessional, and condescending.

Remember, like a tattoo, a quote or picture in your signatures is cute or clever once. The second time it is a redundant and unnecessary distraction.

89

Buzzwords and Trends

It is wise to remain consistently educated on buzzwords and trends within your industry and business in general. If you don't, you may come off as out-of-step or antiquated to potential new clients, staff, bosses, and your coworkers.

You've heard me suggest subscribing to blogs, podcasts, and news feeds that relate to your industry. You should also subscribe to ones focused on technology trends and to those focused on global and regional businesses. You should read business news on a daily basis. So many business owners and professionals do not do this, and it is to their detriment.

Why not use other people's insights to help you be successful? I have been doing this since I was fifteen when I started my first business.

If you work for a company, become an "intrapreneur." There is no reason you cannot use entrepreneurial habits as an employee.

A good example today of a buzzword is "blockchain." The word blockchain is everywhere. People are attempting to apply this term to as many industries, products, and systems as they can, so as not to seem like a dinosaur.

Blockchain is now attached to cryptocurrency, inventory systems, pharmaceutical research, production, and logistics, to name just a few examples.

Will blockchain "revolutionize logistics," "cure cancer," and "eliminate central banks"? We have no idea right now, but the industries that adopt the term blockchain are seen as cutting edge, even when there is no substance to back it up.

Because of its sudden popularity, this term is something we should all be learning about so we can include it where appropriate in our daily conversations. We must also be skeptical and not blindly follow what we read and take it as gospel.

That is why having many sources of news and information that offer divergent views is critical. Don't just gravitate towards content creators with your same political, business, or religious ideology. You will be miss so much! You need to understand the market. The market is full of customers who don't share your views and biases, but they are ready to do business.

The more open you are to divergent sources of information, the more balanced and thoughtful you will seem.

Again, blockchain is a current buzzword. What other buzzwords are you hearing? What do they mean, and in how many contexts have you seen them? Are people using them in divergent ways? Do they seem to contradict each other? Whose definition do you think will win?

Educate yourself about important buzzwords.

Are there buzzwords that apply to your business or industry? Whether it be directly in-house or with your suppliers or with your subcontractors? If so, can you find ways to incorporate them in your daily discourse?

Vocabulary is one of the most powerful tools we have, if not the most powerful.

Business Administration

90

No One Will Care as Much about Your Business as You Do

Thousands of business owners have consulted me for advice. A common complaint among them is frustration with their employees' level of enthusiasm and passion.

Do not expect your employees to match your focus, passion, and commitment. Employees usually want a much more balanced life than owners have. That is why they stay employees.

Your employees are valuable human beings, but they are also tools you use to get your job done. A hammer cannot share your enthusiasm to build a house.

This seems obvious, but what does it mean? Your employees are NOT entrepreneurs like you. Their modus operandi derives from a different place. Just as you need to understand a client's motivations and psyche, you need to spend time to understand your staff's.

If you are a salesperson, even though you are an employee and not an owner, this applies to you as well.

Most corporate sales people are intrapreneurs, entrepreneurs inside organizations, so this idea applies to them just as much as to business owners.

To rephrase the main idea in this chapter for salespeople, no other employee in your organization should have the same level of passion as you do. They are tools to help you succeed.

But how can you increase your staff's passion for your business? Link their compensation to the company's financial performance, meaning they will earn more when you do. If merit will equal more dollars for them in the long run, productivity and efficiency should increase.

91

Staff Missing Deadlines? It May Be Your Fault

This chapter is a natural extension of the last one.

In my office very few people have traditional deadlines. This may sound odd, but if you understand how to hire people and also how to pay those people, then deadlines will be met the majority of the time.

My staff definitely know when projects are due, but they don't have the performance anxiety and the constant feeling of being rushed.

Deadlines have such a negative visceral impact that I don't use the term. Due dates, delivery dates, project end dates, etc. are more friendly.

You want to strive for harmony in your business life as well as your personal life.

Imagine an office environment where you don't have to constantly monitor your employees' project statuses. That is what I have in my office.

You can also have that.

Take a fresh look at your staff members. Are they getting their work done on time without too much oversight? Are you babysitting them? How many of your staff are avoiding you for fear of being castigated?

Turn the focus on you: Are you prioritizing their work correctly? Are you assisting closely enough when necessary? Did you hire the right talent for the jobs at hand?

Take the time now to do an employee inventory—an honest and objective one. Any of your staff who aren't 95% on time with little oversight may need to be let go.

This may sound harsh, but it will be better for everyone if they find more compatible employment.

Now, you can replace them using refined interview methods. Hopefully you will change your hiring process and avoid prior problems. As with any business decision, you need to manage the expectations of your current and new employees much better than you have in the past.

This will save you time, money, and gray hair in the long run.

If you don't have the backbone to make these hard human resources decisions, then you may not be suited to running a department or your own business. Or it might be a great time to find a mentor in this area. That is what I did many years ago.

Leaders must make very hard and unpopular decisions. Management and entrepreneurship are not popularity contests. Decisions must be made unemotionally and objectively, for the betterment of your company and your future.

My firm gives seminars on management techniques in the human resource areas, as well as many others. There is no shame if you have not mastered every management technique! Nobody has. But there is shame in seeing a deficit in your management toolbox and doing nothing to fill that void.

92

Turn Workplace Friction into Team-Building Moments

Unfortunately, today's business environment has become increasingly litigious. Employees are finding more and more ways to sue employers. You need to protect yourself and your employees from potential lawsuits.

Consult with an employment attorney as to what safeguards to put in place to minimize your potential liabilities.

You never know when any subject is going to offend someone, so eliminate non-work discussions when people are on the clock. It is sad, but today it seems that if anything bothers a person it is cause for a lawsuit.

One way to do this is to establish limits and boundaries when it comes to how your employees communicate in your space. These should be part of your policy manual.

As soon as you see employees deviating from these policies, for instance when coworkers are having a loud argument, the first thing to do is get them to be quiet and then get them in a room and go over the policies again.

But if their argument is personal, there is no place for that discussion in the office, and everyone must go back to work. For example, Google was in the news when their internal forums were used for personal attacks filled with invective. This was ridiculous. Work resources should only be used for unbiased collaboration between team members. Injecting ideology and personal judgement of any kind into an office environment should be forbidden. Also, race, gender, politics, and sexual orientation have nothing to do with work performance and should not be mentioned at work at all.

Today, our world is filled with insecure exhibitionists who make constant "status updates" and seek approval about every part of themselves and their lives. That needs to be saved for nonwork hours. New hires need to be told this. The office should never be used as a personal showcase or a forum to seek acceptance of our personal beliefs or choices.

No one at work needs to know about your personal life, nor do they need to approve of any part of it.

Now, back to my discussion about the loud argument. If it was a business-related argument, get the parties alone and find out what it was about. The first thing you must do is reinforce that the employees' mode of communication was unacceptable.

Once you reinforce the policies, allow them to continue their discussion in front of you.

Many people come from dysfunctional homes, have dysfunctional personal relationships, and have worked in dysfunctional business environments. You need to set standards of office decorum and interaction. My approach is always one of nonjudgment, absolute respect, and the desire to maintain everyone's dignity.

Remember everything starts with you and your behavior. You are the leader and the example. Many entrepreneurs are bullies and are loud and aggressive. No matter what policies these types of people institute, their behaviors will be adopted by their staff, similar to how a chain-smoking parent should never be surprised when they find their child smoking in the bathroom with the window open.

You must always remain calm. Imagine you are a piece of granite with a raging river enveloping you. Never does the water permeate the granite; it simply flows around it. The granite is never dramatic and is always consistent and strong and true.

In any interaction, I place more importance on HOW the interaction is taking place than on the topic at hand. Disagreements, friction, and drama are all temporary.

In my office, I try to establish what I call "respectful listening."

The basic ground rules of respectful listening are:

1. You should not be interrupted until you are finished speaking.
2. Establish and keep direct eye contact.
3. Voice levels can become "passionate," but not at a yelling volume.
4. The discussion must stay on topic.
5. There are no mean words or personal attacks.
6. You may disagree on something, but that should not diminish the mutual respect and camaraderie you feel for each other.
7. It is not important that someone agrees with you.

8. If someone does something you don't like, assume they are doing the best they can and that it was not done on purpose.
9. Be sure to not disturb coworkers. Move to a more private area if necessary.

Volatile topics will come up often. They are temporary, and then they are gone. But the method of communication can leave lasting scars. So make sure the communication is always done in a respectful, objective, and sensitive way every time. That way every discussion leaves all parties, even those who technically lost, feeling they were heard, respected, considered, and left with dignity intact.

Many times when I see an employee interaction escalating to a negative place, I intervene and suggest there is a better way to communicate, regardless of what the topic is. All topics are of course "my business," but first and foremost the argument is between the employees. My management goal is to make calm, respectful, and objective conversation the norm for them—to turn the friction and drama into team-building moments.

I stopped many a nasty argument in its tracks this way. I did not take a side, and I didn't discuss the topic being arguing about. Again, volatile topics will come and go constantly in our lives. I learned a long time ago that I cannot micromanage my staff's lives or problems.

I want to give them lessons in self-observation. I want them to be able to control their emotions and their demeanor, which is so rare today. I want to give them healthy communication boundaries and rules they will enforce the rest of their lives, well after they have stopped working for me.

Many times my staff come to me to ask my opinion at the first sign of friction. It is at these the moments when I know my nonjudgmental management style and strict communication guidelines are working.

I want my staff to recoil from anyone who communicates with them aggressively, loudly, and without respect. And those employees who have those negative traits but quickly adopt my style appreciate that they no longer need to be a bully.

If you are an entrepreneur or are a manager in charge of groups, you must be vigilant to remove negative people. They are toxic and breed a hostile work environment where your best people will want to quit. We can never allow this to happen. If they will not see the benefits of my communication style and fall in line, show them the door.

This is a valuable life lesson you and your staff can apply in your personal lives.

In my office, I try to minimize discussions on the following topics:

- Religion
- Politics
- Sex
- Sports
- Gossip
- Personal comments about each other

I do this to maintain peace. We have every right to restrict discussions to work-related topics during work hours and on work property.

Moments of friction and drama can become team-building moments. You can use them to impart healthy social communication skills, and to teach your staff to use those skills and demand them from others. They will thank you for this many years from now, long after they have left your employ.

Maintaining equilibrium and peace in your office ecosystem should be a daily focus and mission.

93

Never Have Your Phone System Say "We Are Experiencing High Call Volume"

Remember to treat every client interaction as if it is the first one. Do your potential or existing clients hear this phrase when they call you?

"We are experiencing high call volume."

What does this say about your company? Nothing good.

What does this say to me?

1. That you have so many complaints, and are getting so many dissatisfied customers calling you, that you cannot handle that call volume!
2. You are saving money on telephone operators at the expense of the client.
3. The customer's time is worth nothing, and prolonged hold times are a cost of doing business with you.

4. We have your money already, there is nothing you can do now, so sit there and listen to this terrible hold music as long as we tell you to.

This is one of the worst marketing/customer service disasters I have ever heard or seen.

Does your company use this message for callers? Do your best to make them change it.

Does your company's phone system answer with an automated (not human) attendant? The sooner a client/customer hears a real human voice, the sooner they feel their needs are being addressed. Yes, they still may have to hold, but hearing a person on the other line brings comfort. An automated attendant is cold, rude, and dismissive.

If possible, return to the tradition of having a human being answer the phone.

94

Eliminate All Sour Milk from Your Organization/Team/ Client Base

Office harmony is critical.

Sour milk needs to be excised from within and without your organization as soon as possible.

As a business owner or a sales team leader, you are responsible for maintaining your corporate culture and society. You have a responsibility to eliminate any negative influences at all times.

So in other words, those who do not play nice at recess get expelled.

You should make this very clear when you are interviewing potential new hires. I often say that your job performance is just as important as your personal and social performance within my organization. So, not only will your work performance be gauged, but the feelings of the other team members will be considered as well.

If you are causing discord, this will not be tolerated. I owe it to my team to make their time at work pleasant, supportive, productive, and fulfilling. We all have to work, but I strive to make a peaceful workplace that my employees do not mind coming to every day. I urge you to make the office environment quality-of-life a daily priority from now on. Although I talk about employees as tools and human resources, they are human beings first and need to be treated with dignity, respect, and consideration for their personal space and well-being while on the job.

If I keep toxic personnel in my employ, I can't blame other personnel for leaving to find a better work environment. I know I would.

We need to avoid this situation. All too often owners and managers are focused on the bottom line and forget there are hard-working human beings, not machines, creating results and successes for us. Those human beings need to be nurtured, respected, and appreciated.

Whether you have your own human resources personnel or an outsourced HR solution, make sure they are emotionally available and personally insightful.

Finding new hires that meet technical requirements is easy. Finding candidates who are the right fit for your culture and social structure is not.

Be sure to include many interview questions that will give a clear understanding of the interviewee's personality, mores, and group and team psychology.

When I interview I ask more social and psychological questions than technical ones. It is very easy to know if someone has the technical skill to do a job.

The same applies to clients. There are times when I need to fire a client because he or she brings toxicity to my employees. So spend extra time to see what kind of "milk" potential hires and clients really are.

If sour, pour it down the drain and move on.

95

Be The Last One to Hang Up

I try to wait for the person I am talking to on the phone or video chatting with to hang up first.

We have all been there. Just as you hit the end call button, you hear the client excitedly remember something they need to ask/tell you.

You'll be surprised how often people have more to say, but we have already hung up on them.

This is a hard habit to break, and I still do this all the time. When we are done talking we naturally hang up.

Remember, we are the least important person on the call, so that means the client will dictate when the call ends.

Try to practice this, and you'll see how quickly you're hanging up the phone sometimes.

96

Check Your Spam Folder Periodically

Gmail has the best spam filter system I have ever used. I urge everyone to use Gmail as your email client, even if you don't have a Gmail account. Many people don't realize they can use the Gmail functionality for email accounts from their place of business or from other email providers such as Yahoo, Hotmail, etc. See the next chapter for more information on that.

We spend so much time going through our inboxes. Finding the right spam filter can save us so much time. But even with the best spam filter, items that are not spam can find their way into our inbox. I start each day with a review of my spam folder, as there may be emails that came in overnight that don't belong there.

I move emails out of spam by marking them as NOT SPAM and then deleting the rest of the remaining items in the spam folder. This gives me a clean spam folder every day and allows me to address emails that were wrongfully put in spam right away at the start of my day.

I can't tell you the number of important emails I have caught in spam.

So take a break from reading right now and check your spam folder!

97

I Hope You're Doing Great!

If you have chat or text-based customer support, avoid using canned and hollow generic greetings such as: "Hi! This is Tina. I will be your customer service rep today. How are you doing? Please know I will do all I can to take care of your issue today! Who am I chatting with?"

Remember, chat windows are small, especially on a phone.

Customers in need are usually emotionally upset and lacking patience. So let's make things as fast as possible. Pleasantries are a waste of time and can make the situation worse. This may sound counterintuitive, but it's true.

This false familiarity and related pleasantries are extremely offensive.

When a customer initiates a tech support or customer service chat, allow them to submit their issue at that time, prior to being assigned a representative. Also allow the client to input verification information so the representative can get right to work when they are available.

In my scenario, the flow is more like this.

Customer initiates customer service support chat.
Customer Number: 2739
Customer Verification Info #1: xxxxxxxxx
Customer Verification Info #2: xxxxxxxxx
Issue: I was promised my delivery today and it did not arrive.
Customer service rep: Got it, one moment.
Customer service rep: FedEx actually had an issue and did not come for the late pickup as usual yesterday. Your package was picked up by them today and is on its way. Here is the tracking number: #xxxxx
Customer service rep: Anything else I can help you with?

Have your support reps working on the issue immediately. Sending canned pleasant responses only gives the impression you are wasting time.

Remember, someone in need and experiencing prodserv issues is the most important person to take care of, and quickly. As I have said in this book and elsewhere, a client with a problem can become an even more loyal client in the future if you handle their concerns the right way.

Any client who contacts customer support is having a terrible day; no need to ask how they are feeling.

These interactions should be treated more like an emergency room intake. Imagine an emergency room surgeon, with a patient bleeding out on a gurney, saying:

"Hi! I'm Joan, and I will be your trauma surgeon today! So nice to meet you! How is your day? My surgeon number is 56473892829. Your emergency room case number is AsDeuyrGG67Bb. I am here to help you. Who am I operating on today? What seems to be the problem?"

The client has flatlined at that point.

98

Have an Office Policy Manual That Defines Dos and Don'ts

Require new employees to read your policy manual and sign an agreement acknowledging its contents as part of their employment.

Here are the basics of mine:

1. Dress code, applies to men and women
    a. Knees cannot be exposed
    b. Clavicles (collarbones) cannot be exposed
    c. Shoulders cannot be exposed
    d. Overly form-fitting clothes should be avoided
    e. No visible tattoos

2. Disallow office discussions about the following topics:
    a. Religion
    b. Politics

   c. Sex
   d. Sports
   e. Office Gossip
   f. Personal matters

3. No commenting on coworkers personal appearance

4. No distracting clothing or accessories are allowed

5. No political protests during work hours

I want to elaborate on my feelings about visible tattoos in the workplace.

I don't think many people realize what the visceral reaction is to a tattoo. It is extremely negative. It stems from prehistoric times. Imagine sitting around a campfire 10,000 years ago when you suddenly see a large discoloration or marking on someone's skin. This would be alarming as it may be sign of disease, infection, a parasite, or some other type of sickness. You would move away from this person naturally and instinctively.

I'm not talking about a small tattoo, such as one on the inner wrist, as that is not constantly in view.

I don't want anything visible on one of my team members that can elicit such a negative reaction. The same goes for bright clothing, pink hair, nose or lip rings, etc. It is the distracting nature of these things that needs to be avoided. This is not a judgment of any kind, just a preference for my office decorum, which stems from being modest and unimposing around others.

This is my office, and it is my right to enforce codes that will ensure I make the right impression.

Imagine how imposing it would be for a coworker to constantly say they are a Yankee fan, and you have no way of stopping it. There is no difference when someone has a constantly visible tattoo with the Yankee logo on it. Okay, I get it, you are a Yankee fan. But having a constantly visible Yankee logo tattoo is the same as constantly expressing it verbally.

Visible tattoos are distracting and have no place in the office. Those outward and visible personal expressions should be saved for your personal spaces. Hire people who naturally want to be unimposing hard workers, who respect the space of others, and who are not prone to stand out for the wrong reasons.

You will read in this book how great your responsibility is to maintain a professional and peaceful work environment for your staff. Yes, they are there voluntarily, but they are forced to work closely with people they would not necessarily socialize with. Remember that point.

Team members/staff should be taught to respect this concept and make sure they are imposing on others as little as possible, verbally and visually.

99

Hiring Advice: Job Requirements Coupled with Culture Compatibility

Just like all other purchases, who you hire must be based on the specifications of the job and not what is currently fashionable in the marketplace. And you mustn't start with the price you want to pay for staff. That is a mistake for any business purchase.

When I purchase new computer equipment, I develop a detailed specification and requirements list and then find the best price, not the other way around. The same goes for staff.

Here are three criteria a business owner should consider when hiring.

1) Does the applicant meet the job requirements?
2) Will the applicant fit into the culture of my business?
3) Can I pay them what they are worth?

Too often human resource professionals and business owners have a preconception in their mind of the types of people they should hire. This is sometimes driven by social pressures or biases, and it needs to be avoided at all costs. Your hiring decisions must be based on who will be able to do the job and who will not be a disruption socially among your staff.

Be open to every potential candidate, of every background, or you may miss the perfect person who can meet your needs.

I have seen many business owners make poor hiring decisions because they limited their pool of candidates, meaning they ignored specific classes of people based on criteria that had nothing to do with the job specifications.

They might feel justified and good about themselves, but at the end of the day this hurts everyone, especially them.

How?

If the new employee is not hired by the rules above:

1. They may not be able to fully perform the work they were hired for.
    a. Now other staff may have to take on extra work to meet deadlines, which leads to resentment and the resignation of top talent.
2. They may not be a good fit for the work culture.
    a. This can alienate existing staff by causing discomfort and discontent, which leads to the resignation of top talent.

You are responsible for maintaining harmony in your office's culture.

Be open to everyone who applies for a position. But remember, you have the right to only hire those who can do the job, fit in, and represent the vision of your brand.

100

Take the Time to Recognize Excellence

All too often today people are quick to complain and slow to recognize excellence.

If I am talking to a tech support person on the phone, and they really were exemplary, I will always ask to speak to their supervisor and also ask for an email address so I can send complimentary comments.

Many of the managers and business owners for whom I consult and coach have this failing: they are very quick to be critical and not to praise. This creates a terrible environment where the only possible feedback someone believes they can get is negative.

I urge you to take an inventory for a week's time of your interactions with your staff, salesforce, and others with whom you interact in your life. Are you seen as a strict taskmaster? What is the tenor of your words?

Every day I make it a point to tell someone how much I appreciate them and why.

Some managers tell me, "Hey, my staff are supposed to do their work and do it correctly!" Technically true, but feedback always helps, especially when recognizing a job well done.

101

Maintain Peace and Calm in Your Business Space / Minimize Audio Distractions

You owe yourself and your employees/team a peaceful work environment. This will allow them to be their most productive. I strive to have a stress-free office environment so that employees will not mind coming in.

I often ask my staff for ways I can improve their office experience.

These are some types of things to avoid in the office to maintain optimal performance:

1. A sad, tense, or anxious person who exhibits those traits consistently.
2. Ringing phones (use vibrating ones on your desks)
3. Break rooms or kitchens without doors
4. Staff who disturb their coworkers with personal anecdotes

5. Loud phone talkers in the office
6. Loud conversations between staff

You should make your office a haven, and a quiet one.

Sad, tense, and anxious people spread their emotional problems like a contagion. They can take up a lot of emotional space and become a dark cloud over their coworkers. Vaccinate your office against this pathogen, and let the sun shine back in.

When possible get phone systems that have a vibrate mode similar to what the cellular phones have. I cannot stress enough how distracting it is to have multiple phones that can ring all day. There is no need to have phones ringing.

People can congregate in kitchens and break rooms. That is the space to have light discussions and to relax. But make sure there is a door so as not to disturb their coworkers out on the floor.

So often I see employees who act as if they are hosting a late night television show. They seem to have a limitless supply of inane stories. They believe they are funny, and that everyone loves their "show." If you have one of these, do everyone a favor: cancel it.

Are you that person? Self-observe over the next few days and see how much time you spend bothering coworkers with personal stories. Eliminate that during work hours. Your coworkers, who have been painfully and politely listening to you, will be so relieved.

Allow people to have soft music playing at their desks. I am not a big fan of having piped-in music throughout an entire office. But that all depends on the type of office you have. For example, a dentist or a doctor who has examination rooms and a reception area may be enhanced by having piped-in music with speakers in the ceiling in every room. But when you're dealing with a large office with many cubicles, sometimes that can be very annoying to staff members. A better suggestion is to allow them to quietly play their own music at their desks with speakers or headphones.

If you have loud talkers, they probably do not realize it. It doesn't take long to get them to lower their volume for the sake of everyone else. If you can be heard two cubicles away, you are talking much too loud.

102

An Alarm That Is Always on Is Quickly Ignored

"Business alarms" are important tools. But to be effective, they need to rarely go off. Are yours going off too often?

Remember, we evolved to ignore sounds and sights that are consistent in our current environment to help us survive.

I call this adapting to the "Pace of the Room." What does this mean?

Have you ever realized you can be in a perfectly quiet room or on a loud subway platform, and your ears adjust so you can continue a conversation?

The "Pace of the Room" has changed, in this case, the noise level, but we can still function perfectly.

An alarm that continually goes off quickly becomes part of the background noise, similar to that subway platform noise, and its impact and correct use is lost.

Are your business alarms going off so often that they are fading into the background? Then you may need to reevaluate them.

Again, alarms are very rare in my world. "Fires" erupt infrequently. The better you plan your work and anticipate pitfalls, the less you will hear alarms.

Do you find there are too many emergencies causing too many alarms in your business? Take the time to perform a full-system check and reevaluate all alarms from scratch.

103

Replicate Your Systems and Train People on Them to Increase Growth

Many of my clients are entrepreneurs, and some of them have control issues.

This is not a criticism. Controlling their environment and themselves are two keys to success for entrepreneurs. As an entrepreneur myself, and being the main responsible party of my firm, I strive for these. But I find that many of my clients do not train others and make them independent enough to sell or produce on their own.

This of course holds back their growth.

Replicating your systems and methods by training others does take time and cost money, but remember my adage: "An ounce of training equals a pound of profit."

You cannot do everything, but if you train the right candidates, you replicate your accumulated genius and can exponentially increase your profits.

Along these lines, try to discover companion products or services to sell. Is there another company that offers a complementary prodserv that you could also sell and make a commission on?

Another benefit of codifying your systems is that your firm's' marketability and value will increase, in the event you want to sell. To expand on this, if it seems you are too vital to the go-forward of your company, how can you sell it and retire? Many times you can't, or you need to sign a long-term agreement to stay on as a consultant. That doesn't sound like retirement to me.

Another idea to consider: What if your intellectual property and proprietary systems could be used in a different profit center? You might make handbags, but what if you could take the same systems and methods and make shoes? Either way, empowering someone else with your knowledge will allow them to take the reins of that new division.

Don't be afraid to share your secrets to success. If you have intellectual property concerns, then talk to an attorney about preparing employment and noncompete agreements to protect you.

If you don't share your methods and systems, your financial success will be limited.

Take a moment and be honest with yourself. Are you overly controlling your staff and their communication? Are you being a "helicopter boss"?

Do your clients feel you are the only person they can talk to for important answers?

The fear of clients leaving you when a staff member quits is real, so I understand wanting control. But, in the long run, the number of clients who might leave in those situations is small, and the profit that is lost by overly controlling things is enormous and outweighs that small potential loss.

Talented staff who are not empowered to reach their full potential and fully participate in your company will leave.

104

Double Your Typing Speed!

Learn To touch-type and buy a mechanical keyboard. If you currently just hunt and peck when using a keyboard, I cannot more strongly urge you to learn how to touch-type. This means to fluidly and quickly type without looking at the keyboard.

I find the younger my clients and staff are, the less likely they have this skill.

I cannot tell you how much time you can save if you learn how to properly touch-type. There are so many resources online and in bookstores to learn how to type in a traditional way.

Once you learn to touch-type, I urge you to buy a mechanical keyboard. I only use mechanical keyboards. Research what they are, and do yourself a favor and buy one.

There are different types of "switches" on them, and some are louder than others. They will improve your typing speed and accuracy and reduce fatigue.

Everyone in my office uses a mechanical keyboard. We discard the cheap keyboards that come with most computers.

105

Your Office Computers Should Never Be Used for Staff's Personal Browsing

I recommend extreme restrictions on the personal use of office computers by staff. This is not meant to punish them, but to try to minimize the chance of your computer networks being hacked.

Only work related to my business is allowed on my main network. No personal browsing or email is allowed.

This is not to say that staff should never do any personal browsing at the office. That would be ridiculous, but we can set up safeguards for this instance.

Set up a "guest" Wi-Fi network on your router. If your router is not that sophisticated, buy a new one. A guest network can be electronically separated from your main office network. Allow staff and clients to use that guest network for personal devices that need an internet connection.

I keep some Chromebooks on hand in case a client or staff member needs to log on for something during a meeting or during the day.

Learn about whitelisting and blacklisting. In brief, this will allow you to filter the internet information flowing into your networks, and allow or disallow certain websites, terms, etc.

For example, you could disallow terms or content you find offensive, such as:

"XXX"

"Pornography"

"Sex"

You can block domains completely. For example, you may want to block websites that are not used by your business and that can be a temptation for staff to log into on your computers:

www.facebook.com

www.amazon.com

www.nytimes.com

Many people don't know how powerful some of these tools can be. If you are responsible for a network or rely on one to do your job, I urge you to implement some of these controls as soon as possible.

Hire a network security expert to evaluate your systems and make recommendations to enhance your security.

106

Institute Internal Controls and Fraud Deterrents in Your Accounting Systems

As a CPA, I am often asked to review accounting systems for vulnerabilities. No matter what your business size, I strongly suggest you hire a CPA to do the same.

Hiring a street-smart CPA is a great first step. Remember, though, many CPAs, even though they own their own practices, are not entrepreneurs. They may be technically skilled and able to prepare income taxes very well, but that is only a small part of the expertise a CPA can provide for a business.

Do you currently have a CPA? Are they up to the task of helping you manage your growing enterprise? Be very honest here. Many companies outgrow their accountants and attorneys. If necessary, interview new CPAs and be tough on them. Ask them for solutions to accounting, business, and tax scenarios. Put them on the spot. A seasoned CPA will be able to answer you with confidence.

Ask for references, and be sure to call all of them. Make sure your CPA is a business expert and a real entrepreneur, not just a technician.

Have a professional review done of your internal controls, and implement recommended changes given by your CPA. Also introduce your staff to your CPA, and let your staff know the CPA will have access to all company records at any time. This alone is a great fraud deterrent.

Learn about things like separation of duties and agency.

And remember, giving others signing authority over your accounts is usually not necessary.

Here are some of the areas where fraud can be taking place:

1. Loans to partners/shareholders is a common way for unscrupulous partners to drain a company's cash over time. My firm sees large sums of money here. Always look for an actual loan agreement with specified terms, and see if there were ever ANY monies repaid. Many partners, especially silent ones (not working in the company day-to-day) do not pay attention to this. These loan balances can grow each year in silence.
2. Business credit cards: There can a great amount of fraud when everything and anything gets purchased by the business. Do all parties involved know what is being purchased with these cards? Are there specific agreements in place that include very specific wording about restrictions on purchases signed by any credit/debit card holders?

3. Company Cars: Is the correct portion of personal use being included in a W2 as part of compensation? Remember, commuting to work is not a business deduction. Auto expenses can be significant; making sure that personal use is billed back to the drivers of the cars is important.
4. Vendor payments: Demand a list of the vendors who regularly get paid, and periodically review expense payments and related detailed invoices to see if any mystery vendors appear. It is very easy to sneak a payment through for a personal purchase and expense it illegally through the business. (I have seen personal mortgage payments, swimming pools, kids' tuition, etc. get paid this way.) It is also common for phantom companies to be created with credible sounding names, and purchase invoices paid through a business, with the cash flowing directly into a partner's pockets.
5. VOIDED payments: Review QuickBooks (or whatever business software is being used) for VOIDED payments. Our firm has seen this happen many times. It is not enough to rely on the accounting system reports. You need to verify the validity of voided checks by going back to the raw data (bank statements and canceled checks). We have seen dishonest bookkeepers pay for expensive personal items, knowing the canceled checks would probably never be analyzed, and they would just need to forge the accounting system entries.
6. Ghost employees: This is a fictitious person who receives a salary.

7. Draw: We have seen issues where partners or owners do not have written restrictions and distribution limits.
8. A lax business agreement can give a majority owner the ability to make decisions without consulting the other partners. What specific restrictions, if any, apply to the majority owners in your business or investments in which you are involved?
9. If the promised returns on investment seem too good to be true, they probably are.
10. Even reasonable-looking investment returns can be problematic; always insist on detailed documentation of the investment, and consider having a professional review that information—even if you have the smallest concern.
11. I have seen many situations where small businesses are slowly being drained by someone on the inside, usually a bookkeeper, and the owners never know.

107

Cashiers Should Always Hand Coins to Customers Separate from Bills

This is filed under a Chris Whalen, CPA, pet peeve. Please, as a favor to me, when your cashier employees are giving change, make sure they never put the coins on top of the bills and then hand them together to the customer.

Customers should be handed coins separate from bills when getting change.

Afterword

If you made it this far, Thanks and Congratulations! Your transformation to Chocolate Milk has begun.

Can you feel it?

I hope that you found some of this information actionable.

I welcome your comments at info@bethechocolatemilk.com.

In *Be The Chocolate Milk* I tried to share all of my worthwhile business knowledge.

Since I was ten years old, when I learned what an entrepreneur was, it is all I wanted to be.

Made in the USA
Middletown, DE
20 September 2021

48673591R00176